Praise for
Unconventional Leadership
and Nancy Schlichting

"The defining challenge for leaders today is to reimagine what's possible in their fields—to do what other organizations can't or won't do, and thus get to the future first. That's what Nancy Schlichting has done throughout her career, and with this insatiably readable and relentlessly useful book, she shows you how to do it too. Nancy is one of the most inspiring change agents I've ever met, an unconventional leader whose uncommon sense can teach all of us about where leadership itself is going."
— William C. Taylor, cofounder and founding editor,
Fast Company; author of *Practically Radical*

"In the early 20th century, Henry Ford took over a struggling hospital in Detroit and turned it into a world-class medical center. In the early 21st century Nancy Schlichting repeated the process at the same hospital, using the same innovative and unconventional leadership methods as my great-grandfather. *Unconventional Leadership: What Henry Ford and Detroit Taught Me About Reinvention and Diversity* tells the story of how Nancy turned around the Henry Ford Hospital and Health System. Under her leadership, in the middle of a global recession and the first bankruptcy of a major U.S. city, the hospital flourished and earned a worldwide reputation for excellence that culminated in the coveted Malcolm Baldrige Quality Award. Leaders and would-be leaders would do well to read this book and apply its lessons."
— Bill Ford, executive chairman, Ford Motor Company

"Our Plan to Win at McDonald's was all about making the business better, not just bigger. Nancy Schlichting has done the same with amazing results throughout her impressive career. This book deserves wide readership for its inspirational look at how to remaster your leadership practices with an eye to the quality of the company, instead of the bottom line."
— Jim Skinner, former CEO, McDonald's

"Nancy Schlichting is an authentic, unconventional, and extremely successful leader. Her willingness to take smart risks and invest in people consistently transformed health-care systems. Moreover, her grit and candor are inspiring. A must-read for anyone interested in leadership."

—Risa Lavizzo-Mourey, president and CEO,
Robert Wood Johnson Foundation

"Sometimes, leading a team to victory isn't about taking the traditional path. Instead, it can take imagination, risk, and the ability to turn obstacles into opportunities. Nancy Schlichting has done this both personally and professionally. I strongly recommend this book to any leader looking to take their team to the next level."

—Mike "Coach K" Krzyzewski, head coach of men's
basketball at Duke University

"In the 21st century, a different type of leadership is required to achieve change that is truly transformational. Leaders need to be flexible, innovative and willing to challenge the status quo to make meaningful progress on increasing the accessibility and affordability of health care. In her book about unconventional leadership, Nancy tells the story of her journey, and outlines what we need to do to achieve transformative change, on a personal and professional level."

—Bernard J. Tyson, chairman and CEO, Kaiser Permanente

"The Ford Foundation proudly carries on a tradition of service and leadership that Henry Ford began almost 80 years ago. I have rarely seen that tradition better represented or articulated than in *Unconventional Leadership*. Schlichting demonstrates that leadership practices can be thoughtful, positive, and courageous without sacrificing effectiveness. This book is a must-read for any leader interested in managing and motivating people for high performance and impact!"

—Darren Walker, president, Ford Foundation

"Nancy's blend of compassion, bravery, and practicality will give all leaders, current and aspiring, the confidence to find and pursue their own form of unconventional leadership. Her strategies will help you to remain resilient in the face of adversity, to the benefit of both yourself and your company."

—Ginger Graham, president and CEO, Two Trees Consulting

UNCONVENTIONAL LEADERSHIP

UNCONVENTIONAL LEADERSHIP

WHAT HENRY FORD *and* DETROIT
TAUGHT ME ABOUT
REINVENTION *and* DIVERSITY

NANCY M. SCHLICHTING

bibliomotion
inc.

First published by Bibliomotion, Inc.
39 Harvard Street
Brookline, MA 02445
Tel: 617-934-2427

www.bibliomotion.com

Printed in the United States of America

Library of Congress Cataloging-in-Publication Data

Schlichting, Nancy M.
  Unconventional leadership : what Henry Ford and Detroit taught me about
reinvention and diversity / Nancy M. Schlichting. — First Edition.
     pages cm
  Includes bibliographical references and index.
  ISBN 978-1-62956-095-3 (hardback) — ISBN 978-1-62956-096-0 (ebook) — ISBN
978-1-62956-097-7 (enhanced ebook)
  1. Leadership.   2. Leadership in women.   I. Title.
  HD57.7.S354 2015
  658.4'092—dc23
                                                    2015032976

To Pam,
who has given me a life I never thought I would have.

To Allie and Nick,
who have added so much to my life.

CONTENTS

INTRODUCTION

Unconventional Leadership: My Personal Journey

My desire to become an innovator in health care was something I thought about and began acting on from a very early age. In fact, I was in elementary school. This was many decades before I led Henry Ford Health System, long before I turned around consecutive organizations in the middle of crisis and recession, and well in advance of my struggle to come to terms with being gay and the impact it would have in my career.

Henry Ford, the icon and inventor, was an inspiration to me when I began reading about great leaders in my early teens. But even before that, I was influenced by occurences much closer to home—deeply personal experiences that guided my thinking and fueled my desire. For me, a trio of events forged an indelible perspective and taught me to think of hospitals as dark, scary institutions, where patients and families were at the mercy of an uncaring system: at age five, I spent a long week in the hospital undergoing tests and evaluations after hardly eating anything for a number of weeks. My grandmother had just died and the sudden loss left me feeling not only frightened and unsettled but also acutely anxious. When evening came around in the children's ward, I was completely alone because no visitors were permitted after hours—not even parents. The rules were absolute and the nurses enforced them with rigid formality.

Later, when I was nine, my mother was hospitalized for a month with a life-threatening condition. It was a rare type of tumor that, although benign, was the size of a grapefruit. She had complications and underwent three separate surgeries. None of the four children in our family, ages two to twelve, was allowed to visit her. We were paralyzed with dread and anxiety, thinking that we might never see her again. When my mother finally returned home, she had lost so much weight that my youngest sister, Joan, didn't recognize her and ran away from her, hiding behind me. Two years later, I remember my father losing his brother and sister on the very same day to unrelated illnesses after both endured chronic hospitalizations during which the information was sparse and the outlook bleak. That experience devastated my father and made a lasting impression on me.

Watching people suffer, with hospitals failing to adequately address the needs of patients and their families, shaped my desire to improve the system of care. I believed that I could do better, and that idealistic desire to create something far superior has remained with me every moment since. Over the years, I came to understand that the situation in health care was much more complex than I realized as a young child. The intricacies of balancing medical standards with financial and fiduciary responsibilities can give rise to conflicts of interest that are difficult to address. However, I also recognized that the opposite was just as true—the problem and solution sets were so elementary as to be starkly apparent. The reality was that health care needed to improve, and to move that needle we had to do things differently.

I set out as a youngster with a plan to turn the established system on its head—starting in the operating room. Surgeons were the most respected, and arguably the most skilled, individuals on the team at the time. They wielded incredible influence. In aiming to be a surgeon, I felt that I would be in a position to help rewrite the rules of health care. However, my earliest training did not go quite as I envisioned. When

I began my undergraduate degree at Duke University, I planned to matriculate immediately to medical school. To my surprise and dismay, I found that I grew weak at the sight of blood, and was not equipped to handle the emotional side of medicine. How ironic: I desperately wanted to become a pioneering physician but I didn't have the stomach for clinical medicine!

That first roadblock threw me for a loop—until I uncovered the proverbial silver lining that put everything into focus. I had an aha moment. As I considered my options, I turned to Henry Ford and other innovators and leaders who had captured my intense interest over the years. I realized that there was a business side to health care, and it could be used as a powerful lever to drive change from a place that I never knew existed. Working on transformation from the helm of leadership and operations meant that I could go outside the traditional healthcare sector for business models and ideas that could be adapted and transplanted all across health care. And that is exactly what I have done.

I have tried to take the nontraditional path forward in my career, as chief executive at Henry Ford Health System, and prior to that as a leader at hospitals and health organizations across the United States. In the service of setting a much higher standard within health care, I have developed a reputation for pursuing the unexpected. During my tenure, for example, the health system closed three hospitals and still doubled in size. As a math equation, that doesn't make a lot of sense, but I will show that it happened because people across the organization came to believe that HFHS is a safe place to innovate and do things differently. Together we changed the system for the better.

Unconventional Leadership

In the pages that follow I will talk about "unconventional leadership" and how its tenets have aided me and the teams I have worked with, in turning around a number of organizations, winning the Malcolm

Baldrige National Quality Award at HFHS, and ultimately creating a high-performance health system that is widely considered a model for organizations within health care and beyond.

Unconventional leadership is by far more fun and exhilarating than the traditional route, but it requires courage and a willingness to commit to difficult change. And it will look and feel different in every case. This book presents a mode of operating rather than a template or model. For me, thinking and acting differently was easier because I don't look much like many of the people around me. I am not a typical CEO operating in a traditional setting. I am a female chief executive of a large organization at a time when fewer than 5 percent of top leaders in Fortune 500 companies and fewer than 18 percent of hospital CEOs are women. My colleagues and I operate in an industry where disruption is common, and we reside in a city—Detroit—that has been in the grip of desperate economic decline and social upheaval.

Over a span of thirty years, working at the highest levels of leadership and serving on corporate boards, my tendency to buck tradition has allowed me to see difficult situations for what they are and choose the right levers for making them better.

Even more, unconventional leadership has allowed me to become an innovator in a notoriously high risk, fast-paced environment. I've been through three hospital fires, numerous bomb threats, several financial turnarounds, and a multitude of business model resets—not to mention the life-and-death scenarios I am privy to every day as I work with physicians, nurses, patients, and the entire health-care team to address dilemmas as they unfold. My point is that running a health-care organization—or any large company—is like running a city: anything can happen. I have needed to think differently in order to respond in real time to all of the change and chaos.

With so few top women leaders to turn to for support and encouragement—and even fewer who are gay—I have relied on iconic role models as I developed my leadership style. As I searched for answers over the years, the legacy of Henry Ford, the founder of

Henry Ford Health System, was one of the leadership stories I tapped for knowledge and inspiration. In fact, Ford's example was one of the things that brought me to Detroit and helped me to find a home here.

As a lifelong student of leadership, I have found Ford's business philosophy, known as Fordism, to be more fascinating and instructive than just about anyone's. In my mind, he was as much iconoclast as icon. He was innovative, to be sure, but his influence went well beyond the implementation of mass production. Ford, for example, argued that high wages were essential for both economic and moral reasons. In 1914, he set a powerful precedent by doubling pay for employees on his assembly line in Detroit. In part, the move was designed to address high turnover among workers who found the job difficult and unrewarding. And Ford argued that a higher wage was not only crucial to the success of his business but also good for workers. The $5 a day pay was highly innovative and represented a radical departure from the standard business practices of his competitors at the time.

There are a number of other reasons Henry Ford has become a touchstone for me in business. First, Ford's vision was a game changer in automobile manufacturing and it achieved multiple objectives. Cost-effective cars manufactured by skilled workers earning steady wages revolutionized the industry. Over the span of my own career, I have always looked outside of health care in order to import improvements and ideas. In fact, I have succeeded by applying the current best practices in *business* as opposed to the outdated modes common within health care. In trying to think as Ford did, I believe I have achieved several goals at once—creating a thriving business, improving the patient and family experience, and also making HFHS a great place to work.

Next, Ford was a true innovator. As an inventor, he often reinvisioned something in its entirety instead of simply fixing it when it broke. My father was an inventor as well, and I have always shared his desire to solve complex problems and usher in new ideas; the theme of innovation runs all the way through my work.

Finally, Ford was a noted leader in Detroit during a period of the city's history that included a number of tumultuous moments, including the onset of World War I. Remembering the way Ford managed through crises has sustained me throughout my tenure at HFHS. It informed my thinking as we continued to build the business, with the support of the Ford family, while the surrounding community of Detroit was experiencing challenges such as high levels of crime, rampant political corruption, and economic instability that culminated in municipal bankruptcy. As I tell this story, I will mention Henry Ford because HFHS is an organization that Ford originally built. This is not a history book, but I will pay homage to Ford's legacy because his brave and exceptional example is always on my mind.

Unconventional leadership worked for Ford and it has worked for me. Furthermore, one of the reasons I am writing this book is that I believe that all leaders, in every industry, have reason to reexamine their traditional thinking. Why? Because constant change is commonplace today. Health care is a complex field that is transforming itself from the ground up—from the way care is delivered and how patients and their families manage their health to the multitude of issues surrounding the national health-care debate. And all of these changes are mirrored across dozens of industries. As a result, the traditional rules no longer apply and every one of us needs to challenge and innovate. I hope that my leadership paradigm and tactics for success can help others progress along that same path.

About This Book

I am a product of the '60s, so I believe in change and the power of everyday people to transform any situation for the better. And yet, individuals need access to the right tools to make that happen. The principles in the following chapters are based on the situations I've encountered over the course of thirty-five years as a leader. I am offering advice, based on my experience, so that readers can apply it in their lives, not only as business builders, and as women and men at work, but also across the wider spectrum of situations we all face as employees, parents, and citizens. This book is arranged as follows.

Chapter 1: Risk Rejection and Be Bold in Your Career

When I was in my late twenties I was promoted to chief operating officer at a 650-bed hospital in Akron, Ohio. Elevated above peers who were twice my age, at a time when the company was losing $1 million each month and hospital occupancy was in free fall, I knew that many of my colleagues were dubious about my experience and qualifications. But courage and confidence served me well at that time and ever since. This is when I first discovered how to work with unions and all-male boards and face potential layoffs and a host of other landmines. In this case, unconventional leadership meant forging my own model while so many women of the time were struggling to route around the gender stereotypes that kept (and still keep) them locked out of the executive suite. I will talk about the tools I used to prove myself as a woman rising through the ranks in business, and I will also offer a candid account of several vivid setbacks and how I was able to overcome them.

Chapter 2: Learn to Turn It Around

Before I got the call to join HFHS, I considered accepting an opportunity at a premier children's hospital in Seattle. It boasted an all-female board; the business was growing; and it was a well-funded institution. HFHS presented a dramatically different picture. In 1997, prior to my arrival, HFHS lost money and was draining cash at an alarming rate; there was no growth; and employees and physicians were demoralized. The organization was in the grips of a crisis while the surrounding community of Detroit was experiencing economic instability and massive population decline.

Given the two paths, I chose Detroit. I gravitate toward big, challenging, complex problems, because they present an opportunity to create positive change.

This chapter examines the art of the turnaround. In particular, it explores the reality of turnarounds in tough markets and industries. I have led four organizations safely through turnaround situations, and while HFHS is the best known, each one has been a case study that shows what happens when you put people and quality above all else, which unites teams around better ways of working together. In examining how my own unconventional leadership intersects with transformation, I will describe each of these cases and the tools I have used to succeed.

Chapter 3: Use Quality to Achieve High Performance: The Baldrige Framework

One of my greatest moments as an unconventional leader came in 2011 when HFHS won the coveted Malcolm Baldrige National Quality Award, the nation's highest presidential recognition for innovation, improvement, and visionary leadership. I got the phone call when I was at home on the morning of my fifty-seventh birthday, and in that instant it felt like we had just won an Oscar.

I tell the story of our Baldrige journey for two reasons. First, the account itself is inspiring. It took us seven years to prevail and no one thought we had any real shot at the prize when we applied, during the dark days of the 2008–09 recession and while we were grappling with sharp spikes in uncompensated care. I will talk about what put us over the top to win. Second, the journey itself was instructional and transformational in terms of thinking and doing things differently. In health care, we sometimes pull off the most miraculous surgeries only to destroy the customer experience with poor valet parking, an insensitive manner of communicating, or cold coffee. Every interaction in health care counts. I will describe how our efforts became the basis for improvement and best-in-class innovation across the board, and I'll show that these efforts can be applied anywhere.

Chapter 4: Find the Disruptors in Your Organization— and Listen to Them

At HFHS, I have made a practice of recognizing the disruptive people across the organization—and supporting them. These are the people who have the ideas that will drive change. I have seen it time and again. One such disruptor (our chair of surgery, Dr. Scott Dulchavsky, who also works with NASA) proposed installing public health kiosks inside churches all across Detroit. It was a fairly radical idea—and yet these kiosks have been enormously successful in helping members of the community learn about health and wellness and in expanding our understanding of community needs in Detroit.

Another visionary disruptor partnered with me in creating a $360-million hospital designed to serve as a community center for health and wellness, and that looks and feels like a luxury hotel, complete with gourmet cuisine and a unique retail complex. This, the first Henry Ford Health System hospital built since 1915, was complicated to execute and was initially criticized by some of the media and some competitors, but it has been extremely successful. Now we use its hospitality strategy as a model for all our hospitals, and it has been copied by hospitals around the world.

I will describe many other ways we've innovated, and will explain how and why innovation has changed the game for us. The bottom line is that we've expressly made it a part of the core fabric of our organization in order to counteract the debilitating pressures and inertia that come with day-to-day business. I self-identify as a leader of positive change, and I will show how to create a culture where innovation is a driver of growth.

Chapter 5: Make a Large Company Feel Small

The early years of Ford Motor Company illustrate one of Henry Ford's greatest priorities—to attract outstanding people. He hired a cadre of individuals who shared his vision and would make the company into one of the world's best. I myself began my career in health care directly out of college as a minimum-wage worker, and held a number of jobs between nurse aide and chief executive. The universal lesson I learned from each position is that every individual in an organization matters and all employees need to be engaged in a common vision. I like to say that we treat surgeons just like housekeepers—with great dignity and respect. None of the twenty-three thousand jobs at HFHS is easy, but my mission has been to create an environment where people can bring their best. As the late Maya Angelou said so beautifully: "I've learned that people will forget what you said, people will forget what you did, but people will never forget how you made them feel."[1] I will describe how I put that idea into practice as an unconventional leader.

Chapter 6: Being Different: The Strength of Diversity

Picking up where I left off in chapter 5, I will transition to a related subject—thinking differently about people. Like many CEOs, I have seen firsthand that diverse teams are a staple of innovation and serve as a lever for creating a high-performance workplace. In addition, ample academic evidence shows that diversity is good for the bottom line.[2] Rather than elaborating on that well-established argument, I will focus on my own simple talent philosophy: first, solving complex problems requires bringing together many different types of people. Health care is a complex field, and yet it is not especially diverse in the executive ranks. I've tried to change that. Second, whether you are recruiting internally or externally, it is essential to take risks. Hiring people with nontraditional backgrounds and unusual experience pays dividends almost every time—I will talk about unorthodox hires for key positions that worked specifically *because* they disrupted the norm. I will also explain how I used this same talent philosophy to find and recruit the person who will succeed me.

I will also discuss my own experiences as a gay woman in business, including being anonymously outed and passed over for promotion expressly because of my sexual orientation. Being out in the open for twenty-five years has made me a better leader, intent upon fostering a safe and comfortable environment where people can bring their unique gifts and true selves to work each day.

Chapter 7: Detroit: Partner for Renewal

Over the course of more than a decade leading HFHS, I can attest to one thing, which remains constant even as all else around us is engulfed in change: we are defined by the community we serve. As such, we have a dual responsibility to serve and improve that community. Just as Henry Ford introduced higher wages that stabilized his workforce and gave workers the ability to buy the very cars they made, we have a business and moral imperative to be a resource and partner for the people of Detroit.

The reality we have faced during my tenure as chief executive is a city marked by deep decline and desperate poverty—a situation we work every day to help turn around. In this chapter I will examine Detroit in crisis and our struggle to expand and to attract top talent to America's most impoverished metropolitan area in the midst of the 2013 municipal bankruptcy. I will talk about the city's amazing history and immense challenges—from the founding of Ford Motor Company in 1903 and the city's heyday as the automotive capital of the world, to the race riots, crippling population decline, urban decay, and a debilitating crime surge. I will also talk about the many hopeful steps along the path to future community renewal and economic recovery. Finally, I will highlight the many personal lessons I learned as a leader during Detroit's time of crisis and the ongoing attempts at renewal.

Chapter 8: Face the Future

Chapter 8 explores how Detroit's future, the evolution of health care, and my own future all dovetail. For me, one of the rewarding things about being in health care for so many years is recognizing progress in many areas, including patient centeredness and improved patient safety in the U.S. And yet, we have a long way to go to create affordable care, create effective access to care for all Americans, attain Six Sigma levels of health care quality, eliminate health disparities for many groups of patients, and increase funding for medical research. I will shine a light on mergers in health care and health-care reform, naming my own successor, and the ways that we can do things differently in order to move the needle. I will also describe my unconventional perspective on succession planning and how I see things playing out for me in the future.

It is my hope that the stories in the chapters that follow will be inspirational for women and men who aspire to lead, and of interest to CEOs who have asked how HFHS won the Baldrige National Quality Award for performance excellence. However, more than anything, I hope that all readers will find the advice useful in confronting their challenges and in their search to find their own unconventional paths to change and success.

CHAPTER ONE

Risk Rejection and Be Bold in Your Career

Leadership is exciting because it brings with it so many surprises and curves in the road. As with any extreme sport such as rock climbing or surfing, you need to be mentally equipped to lean into the highs and lows. And it is not just high-level leadership that delivers a dose of personal risk. Simply stepping up to accept greater responsibility, for any of us, requires a degree of confidence and courage.

In one of my first jobs after finishing graduate school and a fellowship, I was the associate director of planning at Akron City Hospital, a teaching hospital in Akron, Ohio. It was the perfect opportunity for me because the position allowed me to interact with a number of different leaders within the hospital and to learn about the entire hospital operation. What I saw was a mixed bag: the organization was filled with smart, accomplished people brimming with ideas and idealism, and they did important work in the community. But I also saw waste, inefficiency, and a lack of communication as well as an absence of risk taking. There were many departmental silos, an absence of cross-functional teams, and too many people looking to the top for all of the answers.

Then something unexpected happened. The chief operating officer position opened up, and one of my strongest internal supporters urged me to apply. The idea seemed absurd to me at first but the encouragement I received from this seasoned executive made me think. I realized that in this role I could make more of a difference at the hospital, and the possibility lit a fire under me. With a level of confidence and self-determination that surprised me, I wrote a letter to the CEO outlining my strategic vision and making the case for why we would make an excellent team. After a week with no response, I wondered if my bold move would prove to be career limiting! At last, the CEO called me in. We talked for hours about how we could create exciting plans for the hospital. To the shock and surprise of virtually everyone on the leadership team, I was hired, and I found myself managing my former boss and a slew of other excellent people who had decades more experience than I did. That experience launched my journey as a leader and taught me my most valuable career lesson to date: when it comes to becoming a leader, courage is one of the very best levers for personal success.

Before outlining my leadership philosophy, informed by Henry Ford and my experiences in Detroit, I will talk about how I came to be an unconventional leader. The path I took is relevant for a number of reasons. First, I hope that it will provide inspiration to younger leaders. Often, the people I meet ask how I came to lead a 23,000-person organization and manage a number of turnarounds. They, and others, are hungry for diverse role models, and I hope that I can offer something that fires them up to lead. Next, I have been a student of leadership for as long as I can remember, and the trends and takeaways from my career translate into practical advice for anyone who aspires to lead. Finally, I look at the important and valuable *Lean In* movement that Sheryl Sandberg has pioneered and I see that every person's path to success is vastly different. I have leaned in for nearly all of my life, but I recognize that not all people have the same outlook and objectives that I do. Yet, leadership reaches far beyond business and into communities, schools, churches, homes, and families. I hope that the model I have set as an unconventional leader shows people in all walks of life that leadership is everywhere. It is everyone's job to lean into it in some way, shape, or form. Let me begin by telling you how I have done it.

First, the Facts

My career in health care began when I was a teenage volunteer working at Akron City Hospital in Ohio. I wanted hands-on experience, and Akron was the only hospital in the area that allowed fifteen-year-olds to volunteer. Right off the bat I tested the boundaries of what student volunteers were usually permitted to do. I was assigned to the surgical suite with the doctors and nurses, assisted in the recovery room, and provided information to families in the waiting area. The director of volunteers was my advocate at the time, in part, she said, because she saw something distinctive in me—perhaps I was more mature than some other kids my age and I was certainly more focused than most. But the real differentiator was that I stepped up and asked for more responsibility than my peers. I had been waiting for years—since my mom's illness when I was nine—to get into a hospital and really learn. Being proactive gave me a head start that advanced my career.

Right after college, I worked in radiation therapy at the Duke University Comprehensive Cancer Center. I still remember the names of many of the patients we cared for, and the experience forged and framed the way I think about the idea of courage. I saw how patients persevered to conquer their fears and also how they helped one another cope with uncertainty. More than anything, working with cancer patients renewed my appreciation for life and reinforced my belief in the human spirit. If these patients could look death in the face and continue to fight, and even support one another, then I should be able to proceed full speed through my life and career without being blocked or stopped by trepidation or uncertainty.

I was there for a year before starting in the MBA program at Cornell. I was fortunate (and somewhat amazed) when I was later selected to do my administrative residency in New York at Memorial Sloan Kettering Cancer Center. I was born in New York City, so it felt a little bit like home to me. Within two weeks of starting, at age twenty-three, I became the on-call administrator for nights and weekends. It was a bit frightening, but also thrilling, to step up and be handed that level of responsibility. More than just courage and a steady hand, success in the position required a lot of training and support. A number of the people I worked with there, many of whom mentored me, are still my good friends. From there, following graduate school, I went to Chicago as a fellow for the American Hospital Association and the Blue Cross and Blue Shield Association. I worked with the CEOs of both organizations and gained a unique grounding in national public policy and the differences between the delivery system side and the insurance side of health care. The experience fueled my interest in problem-solving innovation, and since that time I have gravitated toward places that had a stake in both the delivery and financing of health care. That fellowship also gave me my first experience reporting to two chief executives and an understanding of the politics of management.

It was during my fellowship in Chicago that I met Gail Warden, who was the COO of the AHA and later president and chief executive officer of Henry Ford Health System from 1988 to 2003. Gail, who became my longtime sponsor and advocate, took an interest in me and after my fellowship suggested that I go back to Akron City Hospital to work for Al Gilbert who was a classmate of Gail's at University of Michigan. He believed Al would be an excellent mentor to me—and he was absolutely correct. With that, I returned to the place that gave me my start at age fifteen. It was in Akron that I learned to promote myself at the risk of rejection. Hired as assistant director of operations (serving one year) and then associate director of planning (serving two years), I took a flyer and applied for the COO job. I wrote Al Gilbert to make my case, and that letter, with its compelling message, earned me the job.

It was an incredible leap of faith by Al—an act of courage on his part that I will never forget.

There were numerous firsts for me in Akron over a period of five years: my first critical turnaround situation; my first major cost-reduction initiative; my first chief operating officer role. It was also the first time I needed to scramble to change minds and secure support from a broad group of leaders within the organization.

When I went on to Riverside Methodist Hospital in 1988, when I was in my early thirties, I was a little more seasoned and a lot more grounded in professional experiences and crisis management. Riverside Methodist, located in Columbus, Ohio, was part of a system of hospitals, and I was recruited as chief operating officer of a one thousand-bed teaching institution that employed six thousand people. I was later promoted to president and then CEO. I was there for eight years, with never a dull moment. Riverside Methodist represented my second financial turnaround, but this hospital was financially stable and located in a city that, unlike Akron, was a growth market. Even as we drastically cut costs, we did a lot of major construction to grow the hospital. All the while, I grappled with extreme corporate politics, personal life challenges, and dramatic lessons about organizational culture.

There is more to tell about these times, and I will do so as we explore turnarounds, continuous improvement, and creating a culture of innovation—among the other topics that recur throughout the book. The fact is that all of these experiences eventually brought me to Henry Ford Health System as chief executive—the most significant and long-held leadership experience of my career.

Before I continue, I want to discuss the challenges in my career— the bumps in the road and the times when, frankly, I wondered if I had lost my way as a leader. Without these challenges, I never could have mustered the courage and confidence to do the work I have done, together with so many great colleagues, at Henry Ford Health System.

Obstacles Along the Path to Success

The reality is that we all must clear the hurdles that rise from our career paths. The confident choices that I have made in my career—stepping up, striving to turn around businesses, and taking risks with jobs—all occurred largely because of the adversity in my life, not despite it.

Being a woman—perhaps a bit less challenging in big business today—was a massive obstacle when I was rising through the ranks of organizations in the 1980s and 1990s. Now, with just 4.6 percent of S&P 500 companies being run by women,[1] the statistics are still pretty grim, but they were even more sobering when I was starting to run hospitals and health systems decades ago. In fact, health care as a sector was dominated by men, especially in administration and clinical medicine—everywhere except nursing and human resources—until fairly recently. I have worked hard to change that in my own organizations, particularly at HFHS, where we went from two women in senior leadership to sixteen over a twelve-year period.

Still, I readily admit to running up against roadblocks and gender stereotypes. When I was looking at grad schools, for instance, I was told point-blank by one administrator to forget about his alma mater. "Don't bother with the University of Florida," he said. "You'll never get in because they don't accept women into the program." I was shocked, but I was on the path to Cornell by then anyway. Later, as one of just two women on corporate boards at Walgreens and First National Bank of Ohio, I witnessed firsthand the challenges women face in both having their voices heard and being granted pay equity. I have never succeeded a woman in any of my top leadership roles, and there have been a few instances where male direct reports had a difficult time reporting to me as a woman. Even at HFHS, I had to ask the board to increase pay for female executives in order to ensure parity with their male counterparts, which they fully supported.

Based on my experience, and on what people have said to me over the years, I know that the bar was higher for me because I am a woman. In order to move up into leadership, women needed to be better than their male counterparts. In some ways, they have had to be perfect. But rather than resenting that, I decided to accept it until I could effect change with my own authority. Perhaps my willingness to take some of the heat myself has helped other women along the way. In addition, I should note that it was always men—mentors and managers—who promoted me and gave me the chances I have had to succeed. Many people took risks on me, and that always made me feel even more committed to making bold career choices and doing the job exceptionally well.

Even more than being a woman, being gay has been the bigger career challenge.

I was nineteen when I first realized I was gay. No one knew—not even my family. I found this part of my life tremendously difficult to navigate: I did not know how to come out to people. There were no gay role models at the time for me to turn to, and I found exactly one relevant book at the Duke University bookstore when I went looking for answers. So I kept my feelings mostly inside, rationalizing that my sexual orientation could be kept private. It remained largely hidden for decades.

Finally, another person's hatred and prejudice forced me to become more open. When I was COO of Riverside Methodist Hospital, the largest hospital in Columbus, an anonymous letter was sent to the CEO of the health system and all of the trustees of the hospital. Essentially, it said, "Congratulations on hiring a lesbian to run your hospital." The chairman of the hospital board, Jack Chester, was a prominent attorney and former White House counsel to Richard Nixon. He was also a longtime friend and supporter of mine. He came to me and said, "Nancy, I got this letter. Is it true?" I said it was. He asked me, "What do you want me to do?" I said, "Whatever you think you should do."

After we talked, Jack called all twenty-six board members personally and said: "You might receive a letter. It is true, but this is not an issue for me." After that, the matter died down for a while, despite one board member who was opposed to my leadership position at the hospital based exclusively on my sexual orientation. Within a year, I was promoted to CEO of the hospital, over the objections of that board member. Subsequently, this individual became chair of the board for the entire health system. The situation came to a head several years later when I was first in line to run the entire system. It was a tremendous opportunity for me and I was the most experienced candidate; having successfully led the flagship hospital, delivered AA credit ratings from Moody's and Fitch, and raised patient and employee satisfaction to record levels, I was on top of the short list. But the chair stepped up his rhetoric once again. In addition to being the chair of the board of trustees, he was also a very large donor. Before the decision was made, he played his best and last card, telling board leaders, "If you follow through and she gets promoted, I am not giving this health system another dime."

I stepped away from the situation despite significant employee and physician support without causing any public embarrassment and left the hospital six months later without a next job waiting. I was unemployed for the first time in my life and I felt humiliated and shell-shocked by how it all went down. Having always kept my nose to the grindstone, and having focused on results over politics, I had never experienced anything like that. It was the worst time in my life in a number of ways. My mother was dying of cancer, I'd left a job I loved, and I was forced to abandon my career aspirations simply because I was gay. But I wouldn't change what happened in Columbus because it is part of what made me who I am today. I took some time off to reflect and regroup. I resolved to stop hiding my sexuality and raise my head high to become a role model for others in the LGBT community.

The experience in Columbus was just a speed bump. And it fired up my resolve and led me to greater things. After a short stint in Philadelphia as regional president running eleven hospitals in six states for the newly formed Catholic Health Initiatives, I was asked by my mentor Al Gilbert to return to Akron to succeed him as CEO of Summa Health System (a three hospital system with a health plan and flagship Akron City Hospital) following his retirement in two years. I accepted that wonderful opportunity, but only stayed eighteen months, because I received an unexpected call by Gail Warden, who asked me to consider coming to Henry Ford Health System as his potential successor when he retired in a few years.

Being a woman on the rise in a male-dominated domain and being a closeted lesbian running Catholic hospitals represent two pieces in a larger puzzle of experiences that made courage and confidence mandatory for me. These experiences are also part of why I am considered unconventional—because I'm different, and I have come to see that as a major advantage. My differences have given me license to depart from business norms and traditions that are no longer effective. Despite the fact that no two journeys in leadership are ever the same, I have thought a lot about success and believe that I have advice to offer people who may follow in my footsteps. We will go much deeper into lessons for executives and organizations throughout this book. In the meantime, we will drill down deeper into career advice that is broadly applicable.

How to Do What Is Difficult

All of my thinking on career success can be summed up in one piece of advice: do the things that are difficult.

My specialty has always been tackling tough tasks, in part because that is what has kept me engaged and thinking creatively. I chose to play the violin when I was eight years old because it seemed the hardest to me—and I still play it today. I went after the COO job in Akron at age twenty-eight because it was a new challenge for me in terms of difficulty. Even choosing HFHS over Summa was the more difficult option of the two. Akron was my hometown, after all, and I had worked there in the past. I had friends and family close by, and it was comfortable and less complex. I was being brought in by my longtime mentor to a place where the financial outlook was relatively stable. Working in Akron would have been an honor, and I could have done meaningful work and stayed put for the rest of my career. It was the easier choice.

HFHS presented a starkly different picture. The organization was inherently solid; it had an outstanding group of physicians and an excellent board. But HFHS was losing money, the flagship hospital was in serious financial jeopardy, patient admissions were not growing, and employee and physician morale was poor. The organization was in crisis, while metro Detroit was experiencing widespread economic instability.

Given these two options, I would choose HFHS every single time. I gravitate toward challenging, complex problems because they present an opportunity to make things better. It may be easier to coast into safe situations, but that doesn't move the needle. In fact, the easy parts of a job tend to concern me because challenge is what helps me work hard and test my thinking. Unconventional leadership means moving away from what is obvious and easy.

In my view, there are four ways people can succeed on their own terms, even as they are doing what is difficult.

1. Be a Student of Leadership

I tell people to worry less about money and specific titles in their career and more about landing in a position where they will learn as much as possible and work with great people. With that in mind, I watch people all the time and examine their skills to see what I can learn. Early in my career, when I was at Memorial Sloan Kettering Cancer Center in New York City, one of the executive assistants stopped me and said, "Nancy, watch how Glenn Wesselmann runs a meeting." Glenn was my predecessor for my administrative residency, so I was especially interested in his career path. I watched him and I was amazed by the way he was able to deftly draw people into a discussion and steer critical conversations. I took note, and today I still use techniques in meetings that I picked up from Glenn. Over the years, I have come to recognize that every leader brings something different to the table and it pays to notice skills that you can add to your own repertoire.

Al Gilbert, my mentor and advocate in Akron, was someone who taught me a lot. Al had an amazing ability to work collaboratively with doctors. Many people on the business side of health care complain about physicians—it's the classic divide between the clinical and business side of medicine. I first worked with doctors as a volunteer many years ago, and I saw the imperative of having good relationships with clinicians. Thanks to Al, I understand the importance of relating to doctors on a more personal level. Getting to know the people who can help me learn—whether these are physicians, nurses, board members, community leaders in Detroit, or experts out in the world—has been a hallmark of my career.

I have a number of role models from history, Henry Ford being the touchstone I always return to. But studying contemporary leaders is just as critical, because you can see them in action and become acquainted with their approach to leadership. Mentors like Al and Gail were pivotal in my career, and were especially significant because there were so few female or gay role models I could turn to. Several Ford family members here in Detroit, as well, have helped keep me connected to our founder. But I have also looked up to people like Elizabeth Dole, who went to Duke and was U.S. secretary of transportation and secretary of labor before going on to lead the American Red Cross, and Juanita Kreps, a Duke professor, who was secretary of commerce and only the fourth woman ever to hold a U.S. cabinet position.

My mother was also an important role model in my life, in addition to being my earliest and staunchest advocate. She was a fashion editor in New York in the 1940s and later became a high school teacher. More than anything, she wanted to overcome traditional gender stereotypes in her work, but she never succeeded to the degree she had hoped. She quit teaching right around the time her mother died. She had three young children at home, her babysitter quit, and of course it was 1960, so there wasn't much support for a mother who was married and wanted to work. But she never acknowledged to me or my two sisters, as we were growing up, that there were career barriers for women. She did not want us to think that we had limitations. As a result, I don't ever remember thinking I couldn't do something.

Interestingly, I am also frequently drawn to the lessons I can learn from the least likely suspects—curmudgeons, critical personalities, and people who are hard to please. There are several benefits to consorting with "difficult" people. First, they think differently than most, so there is always something distinctive to glean from them. Next, they are experts at pointing out flaws and seldom sugarcoat or euphemize. They tell it like it is. Finally, learning how to work with difficult people is vital if you're going to be an unconventional leader yourself. You need to get comfortable with naysayers and work hard at the art of winning people over. Try it and you'll see what I mean.

2. Get Out of Your Comfort Zone

Doing difficult things means taking chances. I have talked about how I've done it with career choices that entailed some personal risk. Another way to move out of your comfort zone is to become proficient in the skills that are daunting to you.

Finance, for example, is an arena where many rising leaders feel out of their depth. Early on, I identified finance, accounting, and operations as areas to explore and conquer. I was uncomfortable with them at the time, but they have since become the most critical competencies I have beyond my people skills. During my MBA at Cornell, I had my eye on hospital administration and I swiftly added an accounting focus. As a woman, I saw that I needed to master the numbers in order to be taken seriously. The financial acumen I gained helped build my confidence and enabled me to go toe to toe with chief financial officers and number-crunching board members, who were mostly men and much older than me. Operations, now my lifeblood, was also totally foreign to me at the time. There were people who told me to stay away from operations because it might become my entire career. But I saw that it would help me learn the business faster and, again, give me opportunities to work directly with the board and CEO on strategic planning. The bottom line: it's easier to be courageous and confident if you become accustomed to testing yourself and learning the skills that are most foreign and difficult for you.

Another skill I knew I needed to tackle, if I was to be successful, was public speaking. In sixth grade I was assigned an oral presentation, but when I stood up to speak in front of the class, I flopped. It was the worst grade I got in school. I remember thinking, "How will I ever overcome my fear of public speaking?" Ultimately, I chose not to back down. Over the next few years I accepted every public speaking opportunity to confront and conquer my fear. In high school, I joined the debate team, and with the help of a great teacher, Lee Smith, became a champion debater competing at the state level. As a result, public speaking has been a hallmark of my leadership from early on. Speaking, like financial acumen, is one of those skills that can be uncomfortable and difficult at first—but facing your fears pays enormous benefits. If you can be a courageous and persuasive public speaker your chances of becoming an effective leader increase exponentially. But you need to accept that perfecting this skill requires persistence and courage.

The last way to step out of your comfort zone is simply by being honest. This one is the most difficult to do because so many leaders feel they need to have all the answers. I learned to be honest early in my career, and it has paid enormous dividends in creating trust. To be fair, I really didn't have much of a choice. It's foolish to fake it when you are a young leader working with more experienced subordinates. In many senses, they knew more than I did! I had vision and authority but they had the experience.

The first time I supervised six seasoned department heads at Akron City Hospital, at age twenty-five, I said to them, "I'm not trying to do your job. I know that I cannot come close to your level of expertise, but I've learned some things so far in my education and my experience that I think can be helpful."

I brought something important to the table and let other people run with their strengths. Often, people come into a position of authority and act superior, or they take credit for their subordinates' accomplishments, so the parties fail to connect. Sometimes, new leaders avoid obvious but uncomfortable truths, and relationships become awkward. When I went to Riverside Methodist Hospital, for example, there were three people working for me who had applied for my job. One woman, in particular, had been the acting chief operating officer before I was brought in, and perhaps had reason to feel resentful. The first night I arrived I took her out to dinner and said, "Mariam, I don't know why you didn't get the job, but I need your help. I need to work in partnership with you in order to succeed." I was telling her the truth and it completely cleared the air. We had a solid working relationship for the next eight years, and I ultimately made her the chief nursing officer of Riverside Methodist.

Honesty opens the door for better relationships. For me, the challenge was confronting the fact that I was a young woman coming in to lead people who were accustomed to working for older men. I just tried to be up front and show an interest in them and their work. Many of them had never experienced a leadership paradigm in which openness was at the center—and that focus had a positive impact on retention and morale.

3. Surround Yourself with Supporters

Doing what's difficult becomes a lot easier if you have a coalition of people around you who have a stake in your success. I mentioned sponsors and mentors above. Both are not only great teachers but can also open doors. When Al Gilbert asked me to come back to Akron to become his successor, for instance, I might have done just that if he had not been so supportive when Gail Warden at HFHS called me.

Al said, "Nancy, you have to consider Henry Ford because this is a very important health system in this country. And for you to have that opportunity, you need to go there and take a look." He was right; it was a great move for me in every way. Al was such a strong mentor that he made it easier for me to move to a larger opportunity, even though it left him without a successor.

Mentors and role models go a long way, but supportive managers are equally crucial. I often tell people: make sure you have a boss who cares about you. If not, you'll stagnate. As a woman, I have been fortunate to frequently work for men who have daughters. In some ways, I believe that's part of what has changed this country—men with daughters have opened a great many career doors for women. It's more complicated than just that, of course; women have gotten ahead for many reasons. Yet, the support, sponsorship, and mentorship they receive is critical.

The final place where support yields career success is in the personal arena. I'm married and have a supportive family, and that makes it far easier to be confident in myself and keep things in perspective. My partner, Pam, not only encourages me, but also keeps me grounded, providing critical thinking when I need it the most. For me, support at home started with my parents, who not only encouraged me but also pushed me to succeed on my own terms.

Probably my earliest memory is of my mom deciding that I should take the test for early admission to elementary school so my sister and I would only be two years apart in school. I passed (somewhat to her surprise since I enjoyed playing more than books!), and that meant I was younger than my classmates throughout my entire upbringing. Of course, I still managed to get into trouble just about every year. Often, I felt that I needed to prove myself in some way. I stood up for myself with a little too much force.

I was different from other kids I knew, just as I am different from most CEOs. As a young girl I didn't wear pigtails and dresses. I liked boys' clothes and chunky watches. Before my braces did their job, I had terribly crooked teeth, and the kids (and even a few teachers) made comments. It hurt for a moment, but I never really listened deeply to what anyone said. I didn't let negativity or personal attacks affect me because I never wanted to be like anyone else. I had a great deal of confidence in myself, which came from the way I was raised. I was brought up with the notion that everything I needed to succeed was right inside of me. I didn't let adversity bring me down and I never listened to the naysayers. This is part of what gives me the strength to be an unconventional leader. Even when a teacher didn't support me—as happened a few times—I turned to my mom because she was a teacher. She reassured me every time.

My father was impressive and unusual as well. He knew how to cook for the family and he claimed to have changed more diapers than my mom. He took pride in the fact that he had progressive beliefs on gender roles in the family. By vocation he was an engineer and an inventor, with eight patents to his name, and he designed nuclear components for steam generators at the Babcock & Wilcox Company. What I admire most about my father is that he always had a distinctive way of looking at things. He said that inventors solve problems—sometimes problems that most people don't even know exist. He taught me that a problem is not a crisis; it's something that needs to be figured out and fixed.

Both my parents were always on the team of people who supported me. I will forever hear my mom's voice in my head saying, "What are you waiting for?" And then my father saying—"Of course, you can do it. Why not?"

4. Keep Your Eyes on Values

The last thing that has enabled me to break free from cultural norms and do what is difficult is that I've made key decisions based on my values. Making career choices, in particular, with values as a guide creates a solid foundation to build on. Even if you fail at a certain task, there is something substantial that remains intact.

Shortly before accepting the position at HFHS, for example, I left two organizations within a space of eighteen months because the positions were not a good fit with my guiding beliefs. In the first case, at Riverside Methodist Hospital, there was a lack of support for diversity within the organization, and it ran deep. I decided to quit and move on. The next job at Catholic Health Initiatives required constant travel, with little chance to establish ties with employees or physicians or the community I moved to. It was not what I thought I had signed on for. At that point, my priority was to establish roots at an organization and work within a community. In both cases, I made difficult decisions based on my personal values rather than opting for what may have seemed smart for my career in the short term.

I am not an advocate of hopping from job to job, of course.

Everyone has her own goals in life, and these need to be actively managed. Many women and men today, I know, struggle with work–family balance. Whether that means taking care of children or helping aging parents, it's easier to make tough choices when you know what is most important to you. I have never had children "of my own" (although I became a fully committed parent to my partner's children later in life). As a result, I know that I've had an easier time than many other women getting promoted and navigating work–life trade-offs.

For most of my career, work has been my primary emotional, intellectual, and practical priority. Still, I have never taken a job based on money. The result is that my career arc has a solid infrastructure—namely, people, performance, and progress. The related values in work that guide me are: strengthening relationships with and between people; driving operational performance improvement and financial success; growing the business through innovation; and strengthening or supporting our ecosystem and surrounding community.

My mom used to say, "Nancy, your whole life has been a set of building blocks," and she was right. Everything I have done I've ended up building upon in some way—even the things that did not pan out as I expected. This idea of *doing what is difficult* is made easier when nothing is lost and mistakes become lessons. Reading about Henry Ford has reinforced this because he didn't succeed right away as a business builder. He only became truly successful in his forties, with the launch of Ford Motor Company.

The truth is that we all need to find our own way, but having a firm foundation can certainly help. In the chapters that follow, I will present the big building blocks that I have used to turn around organizations and foster high performance over the long term.

CHAPTER TWO

Learn to Turn It Around

We do not make changes for the sake of making them, but we never fail to make a change once it is demonstrated that the new way is better than the old way. We hold it as our duty to permit nothing to stand in the way of progress. . . .

—Henry Ford

Henry Ford Health System is a $5 billion organization with 23,000 employees. That includes a 1,200 member medical group, five hospitals, a 690,000-member Health Alliance Plan, thirty-two primary care centers, and many, many other health-related entities. That amounts to a lot of moving parts! When they are all interacting smoothly, it's almost like watching a major symphony playing its best performance—it's mesmerizing. But imagine, if you will, what would happen if an earthquake struck in the middle of the performance. The music would stop.

This is exactly what has occurred in health care. Historically, incredibly intense inflection points erupt about every fifteen years. These massive shifts alter the rules of the game and altogether change how the business is run. Touched off by new legislation, such as the Affordable Care Act, these dramatic pivots impact payments to hospitals, health systems, and physicians, forcing everyone to scramble and resuscitate revenue streams.

When I first worked at Akron City Hospital, the disruption was caused by the introduction of a new classification system (DRG, or diagnosis-related group) for types of hospital care, which altered the Medicare payment system. And when I joined HFHS, in 1998, we were grappling to deal with the Balanced Budget Act of 1997, which substantially reduced Medicare payments to hospitals. These major events hit academic hospitals especially hard because they rely on federal payments for graduate medical education, physician professional services, and hospital services. But all of heath care is affected when legislation and reform mandate major changes.

By the time I arrived at Henry Ford, I had encountered a number of these strategic inflection points and led the charge in major turnarounds.

At Akron City Hospital, in 1983, for instance, we had substantial losses due to a precipitous dip in length of inpatient hospital stays triggered by the new DRG system in Medicare, mentioned above. When I became chief operating officer we were bleeding $1 million a month and occupancy rates had plummeted from 95 percent to 75 percent at the 650-bed hospital. All of this plus a major recession made for a very stressful time. Families across the region were suffering, people were clinging to their jobs, with neighbors and spouses among the unemployed, and I desperately wanted to avoid massive layoffs. With that in mind, I created a plan to reduce 250 full-time-equivalent employees without a layoff. I sold the plan, including an early retirement plan to the board and was also able to get the union to agree. We worked together, day and night, and turned the hospital around within six months and made $9 million the following year.

At Riverside Methodist in Columbus, the situation was similarly intense. Although we were in much less of a crisis, we nonetheless needed to reinvent our baseline cost structure to improve financial performance. As part of that effort, we went through a period of abruptly removing a significant percentage of the expense across the board. We did so by attacking all cost categories and dramatically improving integration with the larger health system. The cuts were a shock to the system, but we needed to proactively improve the business. In the end, we improved our margins significantly and were able to protect jobs by leveraging attrition and taking a surgical approach to cost reduction.

At Catholic Health Initiatives, my next role, we were merging three health systems into one. There was a lot of work to do, financially and structurally, to integrate operations, reduce costs, and simply complete the merger without disrupting or derailing the entire business. It was a dramatic process that mirrored, in a lot of ways, the difficult work of a turnaround.

Later, when I went back to Akron City Hospital, called Summa Health by that time, the organization was in a deep financial quagmire. I had not been there for ten years and had a lot to learn about current operations. Pretty quickly, I started a process of zero-based budgeting. That micro approach allowed me to learn the ins and outs of the financial structure and to understand how the budgets were being developed. Getting down to basics enabled a lot of fundamental shifts in the way departments were operating and allowed us to significantly improve the overall performance. Once again, we got the organization back to profitability within about a year and put it on a positive trajectory that lasted a very long time.

All of those situations turned out to be ideal opening acts for the massive financial turnaround at Henry Ford. HFHS, because it is so large and complex, tends to take a hit on a number of different levels in times of extreme transition within the industry. We rely on every payment stream known in health care as well as a number of others that we've pioneered ourselves. That type of diversity can be a vulnerability as much as it is a strength.

When I arrived at Henry Ford in 1998, we were in the eye of a perfect storm—a triple whammy. Not only did we, along with the rest of the nation, get hit with the Balanced Budget Act, but the state of Michigan was introducing its Medicaid Managed Care plan at the same time, which meant a $16 million reduction in Medicaid program payments to Henry Ford. On top of that, we owned a health plan—Health Alliance Plan—which suffered a three-year period without premium increases because the auto industry, grappling with its own uncertainty, was putting incredible pressure on local partners, including health-care suppliers, to freeze costs. By that time, the organization had been losing money operationally for years. We were posting positive net income based on strong returns from large-cap investments, but the bull market only masked the fundamental problem. The bottom-line results were weakened because of chronic operational losses.

I came on as the chief administrative officer, recruited by the CEO, my mentor Gail Warden. Gail told me pretty quickly that he wanted me to be chief operating officer—the system's first ever. He knew, based on my experience, that I had a strong operations perspective and was always looking for ways to make organizations work better.

I understood right away that this was a turnaround situation. When I took a closer look, I saw some of the problems that went above and beyond the major industry shifts. First, I couldn't detect a cohesive performance strategy that spanned across the system. Unit leaders were setting goals and managing them in different ways. Next, most of the fundamentals weren't being measured. For instance, we didn't have reliable customer service metrics, and employee and physician engagement measures were inconclusive. Another key piece of the puzzle was our system's flagship institution, Henry Ford Hospital.

Founded in 1915 by Henry Ford himself, the hospital fulfills a vital need for affordable, high-quality health care in metropolitan Detroit. It is an anchor institution of the City of Detroit. Yet, by about 2001, the health system was losing $90 million a year with Henry Ford Hospital hemorrhaging the lion's share. The vulnerability of Detroit was a large part of the dilemma. With the city reporting record levels of crime, political corruption, and widespread economic instability, uncompensated care at the hospital was at an all-time high. And because of its size, if Henry Ford Hospital remained unprofitable, it would be virtually impossible for the rest of the health system to operate in the black.

Just after the first of the year, in 2001, with the gloomy financial backdrop looming large, Gail came to me and asked if I would go over to Henry Ford Hospital as the CEO, on top of my system COO role. I jumped at the chance.

It was a complex calculus but we worked on dramatic improvement in three major areas of the health system: Henry Ford Hospital, the Henry Ford Medical Group, and Corporate Services. Since I was also functioning as the chief operating officer of the system, I was able to work with Dr. Mark Kelley, the CEO of our medical group, also a new leader, and a number of other established leaders, to make decisions about costs and priorities. It took about two years to turn things around. We lost $100 million operationally in 2001, but by 2003 we were profitable. The systems we put in place at that time and thereafter are what enabled HFHS to remain profitable for 11 of the last 12 years running—through the 2008–09 recession—while we were building a new hospital, and as Detroit itself shrank by 30 percent.[1] In fact, even with all of those challenges and initiatives in our wake, 2015 will be the most profitable year in our hundred-year history.

I can't say that I've cracked the code for turnarounds, but what I *can* say is that I know what has worked for me on each of these occasions. First, I will mention the common threads that have run through these turnaround situations. Next, I will offer the four specific steps that I take as I endeavor to fix a failing organization and work, with others, to engage in the ongoing pursuit of going from good to great.

Common Threads of Successful Turnarounds

There are a few important commonalities from every turnaround effort I have managed. These are the imperatives that need to be designed into the strategy to make lasting success more likely.

First, in every effective financial turnaround I have seen, top leadership has been personally and visibly invested in the effort every day.

Not just involved but invested. In the case of HFHS, I put my job on the line during the turnaround when I stepped in to run Henry Ford Hospital myself, as chief executive. Why? To send a clear signal to the organization that this change was a priority—I wanted to be held accountable and to position myself on the front lines of change. A turnaround requires a commitment from every person from the top down. From a leadership standpoint, you have to be involved, you have to be present, and you have to put yourself in the line of fire. In other words, you have to lead.

Next, leaders need to not only make the tough calls but also stand by them, first with courage and then with humility. During a financial turnaround you are dealing with a burning platform. It may seem easier to put off the difficult decisions, but waiting only increases the problem and decreases your options. I remember my boss at HFHS telling me when I joined the organization, "Nancy, you know we're having some difficulties right now, but it'll all be turned around by October." Well, it just got worse. We had to face reality and make the difficult choices. We were not seeing revenue changes that would support the expense levels we had, so we had to reduce labor costs, and we cut well over a thousand jobs. It was the most difficult thing I had ever done.

Beyond taking responsibility for tough calls, such as reducing costs and replacing entire teams, it is equally important to find ways to focus on the people being affected and be present for them. We went to great lengths during that time to treat people with respect, dignity, and empathy. As a result, many came back and worked with us later when we started to grow again. Today, if you talk to HFHS employees, many will tell you, "I left in 2001 or 2002, and I came back about a year later." In fact, when I took over as CEO of the health system, I started to attend employee orientations and my question for years was, "How many of you have worked at Henry Ford before?" Sometimes half the audience would raise their hands. We made *taking care of people* a stated part of the turnaround strategy and it paid off.

Sometimes just showing your own humanity is the thing that is critical during the darkest moments. At the time, I didn't keep it secret that the layoffs were the most difficult thing I had ever done. To make life even more difficult, the month that we had to lay off six hundred people at Henry Ford Hospital, my partner of twelve years walked out on me. The two things together were emotionally devastating, and I made the unconventional decision to be honest about that. In the midst of the chaos I told my team what was going on in my life. I sat down with each of them and said, "I just want you to know that I'm going to need your help during this period in my life because it is a tough time for me." It was incredible how people stepped up. Simply opening up made it easier for me to build trust and enlist support.

The final commonality in the turnarounds I have worked on is speed. And this is pivotal. Every time I've been involved in turning an organization around, or seen it done well, there has been an intense focus on getting what needs to be done completed as soon as possible. Getting results quickly and showcasing them makes change easier. Both times at Akron, at Riverside Methodist, and later at Henry Ford we made the necessary changes and returned to profitability very quickly. We completed the entire financial turnarounds within a year or a little more. That is exactly what we were driving for. When that kind of work drags on, the uncertainty is debilitating. Leaders need to make decisions, communicate them to the organization, and implement the turnaround with little or no delay. People need to be able to see the light at the end of the tunnel and see progress. It's as simple as that.

Steps to Turnaround Success

In addition to the common threads mentioned above, there is also a methodology associated with turnarounds that culminates in prescriptive advice. These prescriptions can be used as guidelines for driving change across an organization or simply as a path for making smaller adjustments as needs arise. Regardless, these steps are based on my experience and are intended to be general advice to build on as opposed to a rigorous model.

1. Create a Partnership Model

When I was promoted to chief operating officer in 1999, after about a year at Henry Ford, I found myself in an unexpected situation—drifting all alone. My job was to manage the operations of the health system and improve the faltering results in the process. Without a turnaround, the organization's influence within Detroit would be diminished and its long-term future in health care would be in jeopardy. It was no small task without partners. I needed like-minded senior-level leaders, especially in finance and human resources—but they were nowhere to be found. Not only did key individuals fail to step up, at times they even stonewalled me when I requested assistance. The first step in a turnaround is putting together a team of people with diverse expertise but shared objectives and vision.

When I realized the obstacles I faced with the executive team, I went to Gail Warden and said, "I don't think I can do this job on my own. I can't even get the basic information about how we're doing." I would ask the system's finance team to give me performance data and I wouldn't get it. I would ask a straightforward question and be met with a circuitous answer. So Gail agreed to talk to the CFO. When he came back, he essentially told me to "hang in there" because the finance officer would be leaving the organization in about two years. I couldn't believe it. I said, "Gail, I don't think we're going to make it. We're draining cash really fast, and we don't have a game plan."

It was a tense few weeks, but Gail and I ultimately agreed that we needed to put together a new team of leaders. The group we assembled was pivotal in terms of generating confidence within the organization, creating transparency, and enabling me to have trusted partners during the turnaround. We brought in a new CFO, Jim Connelly, who was extraordinary from the onset and has been a remarkable leader ever since. He runs HFHS's health plan now but was the system CFO for fourteen years. We also promoted a highly regarded leader, Bob Riney, to run human resources. Bob was key because he brought a credible, positive approach to solving problems and a proactive mindset for addressing weaknesses.

Soon after, when I went to Henry Ford Hospital as CEO, we hand-picked new leaders there as well. Changing the entire leadership team at the hospital was a dramatic move for HFHS and largely without precedent. It was visibly painful for everyone. The leaders we exited were good people who had been loyal to Henry Ford Hospital for a long time. Typically, coming into a new leadership role, I commit to working with the existing team even if changes occur over time. But in this case, we didn't have the luxury of working with the existing team, because the urgent situation dictated that we work in a new and different way quickly. From my vantage point, it would have been much riskier to *not* make the change.

After that, as the turnaround plans were being put into place, the real work began. We assembled an outstanding interdisciplinary team internally, which became the new leadership team at the hospital. We invited leaders from our health plan, including the chief financial officer and leader of system care management, and the head of our management engineering group, as well as a number of other talented leaders. But the real game changer was asking all of the key hospital-based leaders in the Henry Ford Medical Group, including the chairs of medicine, surgery, radiology, and emergency medicine, to join us.

Bringing together people from across the organization enabled a much faster flow of information. Even better, it provided an integrated perspective and uncovered opportunities that otherwise would have remained hidden. At HFH, for example, working with the CFO from the health plan allowed us to see that we were losing significant business because half of our health plan wasn't directing patients back to our Henry Ford facilities. We were losing them to other hospitals and clinics around the market! That was a double hit for us because we owned the premium and yet we were paying somebody else for the care instead of referring the business into our own system.

Creating a new partnership composed of interdisciplinary members unleashed enormous wins, as support from diverse members of the team brought access to fresh insights and better thinking around integration. It also improved morale and gave people a stake in the success of the turnaround.

2. Communicate Early and Often

During the turnaround at Akron City Hospital, in 1983, it became clear that we had to reduce labor expenses. More than anything, I wanted us to pull off the turnaround without layoffs. The city of Akron was in a severe recession at the time, with 12 percent unemployment, and additional job loss was more than most people could reasonably be expected to handle. Working with my team, we came up with a plan to reduce 250 full-time-equivalent employees through attrition, reassignment, and early retirement. People would still be making sacrifices, but everyone would continue to get paid. It was an excellent plan but it would have gone south fast without a well-orchestrated communication strategy.

People were walking on eggshells and rumors were everywhere. In order to put the plan into action, we needed to convince the board of directors and then sell the plan to employees and their union. The board was relatively simple to persuade because board members wanted to avoid layoffs as much as I did. The employees and union were a little trickier. It was important to get everyone aligned quickly in order to avoid pitting one group or coalition against another. The last thing we needed was more internal strife.

Historically, the lines of communication with employees had been limited. Management made decisions in conference rooms and information eventually trickled down, losing bits and pieces in the translation. This time communication needed to be different—because the stakes were so high. With that in mind, I decided to tell all the employees about the plan myself. So we set up town hall meetings around the clock, during all three shifts and also on weekends. It was an open forum—people could ask as many questions as they wanted, and I would stay as late as needed to answer them. It was such a dramatic departure from the way things had been done in the past that employees almost didn't know how to react. Luckily, they reacted positively and the plan was accepted by employees and approved quickly by union leaders. The approach was so unconventional at the time that a local radio station wanted to come in and record the proceedings (I didn't agree to that).

That big early win helped me understand the importance of communication, and I have used the same model again with similar success. Communication has forever been a big part of the success of turnarounds. This is particularly true in a field such as health care, where you don't want nurses and physicians, or even frontline service staff, feeling jittery and passing that vibe on to patients and their families. It would be like boarding an airplane to find the pilots and air traffic controllers standing around talking about their problems with the company—you don't want that. You want them to pay attention to flying the plane. The same is true in health care.

I remember that my father faced a possible layoff when my sister and I were in college. He was working at Babcock & Wilcox when the company ran into financial difficulties. Before the company's plans were solidified, it made public the fact that it intended to release 10 percent of its workforce. With two kids in college and two more in line, both my parents were extremely scared, and their anxiety had an effect on the entire family. I remember thinking how terribly the organization handled the whole thing, and it stayed in my mind as a cautionary tale.

At HFHS, and throughout my career, I have found that people want leaders who can take charge and make tough decisions—but they also want to know what's going on and how changes will affect them. The basic blocking and tackling that I've done over the years has been to set up systems that open the lines for clear communication. In a turnaround situation, that means communicating what's going on, why it's happening, what forces are causing the financial losses, and what has to change. The faster you can tell every individual what their status is and how they are affected, the better everyone comes out in the end.

What's more, having a strong communication plan during turnarounds means that I, as a leader, don't do anything alone. Instead, I work in concert with thousands of people. When employees understand why problems occur and what they can do to make a difference, then everyone in the organization starts to align in the same direction. That is when you see progress starting to happen quickly.

3. Attend to the Culture

One of the most unconventional things we did during the turnaround effort at Henry Ford was to focus on fixing the culture from the beginning—even before attending to the finances. Most organizations look at culture after the fact, once the "hard work" of cost cutting and resizing the organization is complete. But the cultural aspect of a turnaround *is* the hard part. Without that, the rest of the effort is utterly wasted.

At Henry Ford, we started with senior leadership, which is where the ultimate responsibility begins and ends. So we got in a room with professional facilitators and forced ourselves to admit the truth about the problems that were causing our poor performance. In our case, the missing link was trust. That one deficiency fostered a lack of transparency, failure to communicate and collaborate, and all-around dismal morale. It was a bitter pill for us to swallow because the organization takes deep pride in its heritage as an institution built by Henry Ford to serve the community and make it a better place. Luckily, that mission also fired us up to address the dilemma.

At the time, the lack of trust was systemic and only made worse by our size and complexity. We had so many professional groups working under one banner, from physicians, professional managers, and pharmacists to insurance specialists, finance executives, and educators. They all advocated for themselves but had a difficult time connecting with one another. And the most acute mistrust was between the physicians and executives. When financial performance started to slide, the problem went from bad to worse.

What we found was that we needed to rebalance our efforts to achieve a better integration model between business units, with less micromanagement by corporate executives. I've always had the attitude that business unit leaders need to take ownership and run their respective businesses. The corporate team needs to create a corporate structure that fosters collaboration. They also must have a servant-leader model in order to support operations. This puts accountability for performance in the right place, with the business unit, and allows for better all-around teamwork.

In our efforts to address the culture, we realized that the key to high performance by every individual was to create a structure that would make success easier. Operationally, then, we worked on making integration organic and eliminating overlap, and we created a path for ownership and accountability across the business units. These changes addressed a number of the financial issues. On integration, for example, there was low-hanging fruit to harvest: we had two separate corporate offices. There had been an acquisition a few years earlier, and both offices remained intact. Integrating those offices, together with a number of other changes, eliminated significant excess cost. The business units, for their part, took greater ownership of their spending. We made it our mission to help each one figure out where their money was going, analyze their expenses, and line up better support and transparency.

The other major issue we worked on in terms of culture was reducing blame and encouraging camaraderie. That effort started during the turnaround and is something we continue to work on even today. For my part, I try to set the right tone. Not every decision I make is the right one, and I want people to feel safe speaking up to disagree.

For example, we took a pharmacy out of the emergency department at Henry Ford Hospital in order to save money during the turnaround. Ultimately, that was a terrible decision. It's a 100,000-visit emergency department, after all, and we needed that pharmacy on site. People spoke up—loudly—and we put it back.

I told people, "We're going to make some mistakes. We are doing a lot of things quickly. I need each of you to come forward and tell us where we're wrong." They did that and more—they started to step forward with their own ideas for change. Since then, a culture of innovation has flourished and become one of the most important parts of HFHS's growth and identity.

Everything we focused on in our cultural transformation cascaded across the entire organization, with the process ultimately involving about fifteen thousand people. It made every bit of difference in the turnaround and set the stage for a lot of the things I've been able to do, with so many others, at Henry Ford.

4. Invest to Grow

It's easy to pinpoint problems in the worst of times, but it is seldom as simple to articulate a vivid path for growth. I've found that fully investing in growth—from the onset of a turnaround—is as important as taking out costs. For instance, in the same period we closed hospitals at HFHS, our primary hospital grew by 30 percent, we acquired two other institutions, we doubled the size of our community care division, and we grew our ambulatory network by a third. We also increased our nursing staff at Henry Ford Hospital, even as we were taking a close look at costs. This focus on growth created opportunities for people who were displaced and allowed twenty thousand-plus employees to see and believe that the organization had a compelling vision for the future.

During a turnaround, part of having a vision means knowing what to keep even as you are making the toughest choices in your life. We left our obstetrics unit intact, for example, even after management consultants said that we needed to shutter it—it would never be cost efficient. At the time, I remember speaking up in a flash to say, "We are not going to take OB out of Henry Ford Hospital." I had never seen any hospital in this country survive after taking the OB unit out. Not only would that sever a strong connection with female patients, it would also eliminate a core capability. Women come into ERs all the time with obstetrics issues. If we didn't have the service, we couldn't provide quality care to the community. It was a hot-button issue and I had to take on the board. We had some people serving at the time who thought, "If it's a money loser, of course we get rid of it." I made the case that that's not how hospitals operate and it's not how health care decisions are made. It was tense, but we got through it and we still have OB. It's a high-quality service center for high-risk moms, with a neonatal unit that cares for fifty babies at a time.

Another part of our vision for growth was attracting more people to Henry Ford Hospital and reversing patient attrition. One reason bringing patient numbers back up was so difficult was the economic health of the city itself. The Detroit automotive industry in the late '90s, although bracing for disruption in the global economy, was basically holding its own. But the City of Detroit was a different matter. There was very little municipal investment and the population was declining. Unfortunately, few business leaders in Detroit at that time were enthusiastic champions, and it was difficult to find anyone credible who was bullish on the future of the city. This was interesting to me because I had come in from outside and I was the only visible cheerleader for Detroit in my circle. It was pretty discouraging, but there was one notable bright spot. The individual who made a real difference was Dr. Irvin Reid, president of Wayne State University. Irv decided that Wayne State was going to significantly increase its numbers of residential students, and he built new student housing on the Wayne State campus in Midtown Detroit. That brought upwardly mobile young people back into the city. It took many years for us to see the positive effects, but the strategic decision was very important.

For our part, we needed to reengage patients and take steps to prevent them from leaking out of the system. A major part of this entailed working with our own health plan to dramatically improve coordination—we needed the Health Alliance Plan to direct patients back to our facilities instead of sending them elsewhere, as I mentioned earlier. It was a huge initiative for us, driven by Joe Schmitt, former CFO of our health plan, and Tom Groth, who previously ran system care management for our health plan. It was their idea and we ran hard with it. It wasn't simple, however, because we hadn't yet made the necessary investments in the facility itself. The hospital was in pretty bad shape in terms of infrastructure, investment, appearance, and amenities. It didn't look great and our service scores had slipped in recent years as a result.

We needed to show visible signs of improvement on a shoestring budget. With that in mind, I laid out a 30-60-90-day game plan around creating symbols of change that everyone could see. For example, in the first month we replaced the old wheelchairs and stretchers and focused on cleaning and improving our appearance. I took a tour of the building with our head of plant operations (a wonderful manager named Dan Murakami) and we catalogued the problems. We found, for one, that some of the elevators were run on relays that Henry Ford himself had probably put into place. People were waiting on all seventeen floors of the Clinic Building because the call buttons weren't synchronized. We fixed that. We also put greeters at the front doors to welcome patients and guests.

One of the critical lessons learned during this time was that the improvements that reengaged patients also reengaged our employees and raised morale. After that, I took every penny of contingency money that I could get and we did a lot of little things. We had parties outside at lunch with food and music. The front of the hospital didn't look very good, so we gave out flowers and gloves and everyone went out and planted. I remember that I wrote an article for our internal employee newsletter about the fact that it doesn't cost anything to smile and to be kind. Often, for patients as well as employees, it is those moments of kindness and personal interaction that enhance their experience tremendously. Between cost reductions and insourcing, we started to see our financial results improve and we were able to invest further in the facility. Eventually, we put in over $300 million.

Small improvements clearly made a major difference. But that's not all we did to invest in our growth. One of the commitments we made, which completely changed the trajectory of the system, was a major one.

In the early 2000s, the chair of the urology department at Henry Ford was my friend Dr. Mani Menon. Dr. Menon had a dream, and it was a big one. He wanted to use robotic technology to revolutionize the treatment of prostate cancer. Specifically, he wanted to partner with da Vinci, the robot maker, to pioneer a far less invasive procedure that yielded superior outcomes for prostate surgery. After struggling to gain traction with the previous leadership, he came to me and said, "Nancy, I really believe this is going to make a big difference and here's why…" After our conversation, I decided I was going to take whatever risk was involved and find a way to support the effort. But it was big money and a tough sell. He needed to outfit a brand-new operating room with updated technology for robotic surgery. The resources required were significant for us at that time, and it wasn't clear whether this was going to work—it had never been done.

In the end, we funded a large part of the project ourselves, and Dr. Menon also secured a large outside donation. This was a groundbreaking advancement that attracted considerable attention in the medical community worldwide. In addition to revolutionizing care for prostate cancer, the advancement gave HFHS its mojo back. In fact, I credit Dr. Menon and the Vattikuti Urology Institute, in large part, for fueling our turnaround. And all the positive recognition from the medical community for the Institute, together with innovation and investment, brought patients back. At a time when we were unsure people would drive to our hospital from across town, we were suddenly seeing patients coming to Detroit from all over the world.

People at HFHS were enormously proud, and the tenor of the organization changed for the better. Employees started to believe, in effect, "Innovation is being rewarded here. Nancy and the team are taking some risks." And, as the cultural tide changed, the turnaround really started to take hold.

Anticipate the Next Turnaround

The most significant aspect of HFHS's turnaround was simply that we got through it and became stronger than ever. Industry turning points and disruption are going to happen from time to time, and sometimes organizations lose their way—and it's necessary to just deal with the situation head on. The second most significant aspect of the turn-around at HFHS was that we never wanted to go through it again. That mind-set has been a tremendous motivator for managing costs and maintaining our focus on quality and service.

The outside events that started the problems for HFHS in the late '90s were complicated and largely outside of our control, but they didn't happen overnight. The beginning of the end, one might argue, was a failure to anticipate what was coming down the pike. The challenge we all face in health care, and in every other competitive industry from media to automotive, is to gain foresight and be prepared for whatever the future may bring. Yet, prior to my arrival, HFHS did little such preparation. One problem was that Gail Warden, a remarkable leader, had other responsibilities, including serving as chair of the American Hospital Association in 1995, and was often absent. His number two, who had been the chief administrative officer, had left the company around that time to take a position in Texas. There was a gap in leadership and no one was planning for this incredibly difficult situation resulting from the many complex forces described above. As a result, we were losing money.

Henry Ford said, "Before everything else, getting ready is the secret of success."[1] I adhere to that same belief and have put it into practice. After the HFHS turnaround, for instance, we have always paid attention to the potential threats coming at us, alongside our everyday plans and priorities. Recently, for instance, when we began to see some troubling indicators in regard to our financials, I worked with COO Bob Riney to get us back on a cost-reduction path. At the time, we were implementing a new medical records system for the entire system, to the tune of $350 million. Simultaneously, we were dealing with updated Medicare and Medicaid reimbursement changes stemming from the Affordable Care Act. We implemented a three-year strength and sustainability plan for the health system that had a $60 million impact in year one. That's money in the bank, literally.

One thing that has helped me anticipate changes in the landscape is being extremely broad in what I read, in developing networks of people that span industries, and in participating in health-care conversations, both nationally and locally. I'm always scanning for broad trends and watching for what may trip us up. When you do that over the course of a career, you get better at it. You begin to see what metrics are most important—the things that may be devastating to the business if they're left unaddressed.

At Riverside Methodist, we decided to make some big changes because our cost structure was too high. We did this while we were still very profitable because we wanted to avoid the real trouble that would come if we failed to act. Part of what I've done at Henry Ford over time is to introduce what I call leading indicators. These are the things we pay exceedingly close attention to. I watch cash every single day, for example. When I came on there was no cash metric whatsoever, and we went through $250 million in cash in about a three-year period. I thought, "That can never happen again." I also watch volumes like a hawk. If I start to see a decline, I call people together fast and we put a plan into place. What else? While some people monitor budgets, I monitor year-over-year trends. Budgets can be very misleading, depending on whether they're overly aggressive or not aggressive enough. In other words, you can be doing great on your budget and be failing miserably.

Another leading indicator, for me, is national and federal trends—especially in terms of what the federal government is focusing on in health care, including payments and funding. With the high level of poverty and uninsured people in Detroit, we are very reliant on the government for payments. We spend a lot of time advocating and making arguments to keep all of our payment streams in place. We also spend time in Washington and Lansing advocating for what is best for our community. But we always know that the government could throw a boulder in our path around the payment issues. We pay close attention because it impacts our people and our ability to deliver the highest level of care. This is the thing I can't control and it's the thing that can keep me up at night. For the last few years, for example, we have seen that medical education payments are a likely target for federal budget reform. As a teaching hospital, that line item change stands to affect us in a major way. I can't say that we have an effective response just yet, but we are preparing for it. What happens in 2017 if we face a $50 million or $100 million reduction in medical education payments? How are we going to train residents? Are we going to have the same number of programs?

These are the types of things that I keep people focused on—including our boards. There's an anticipatory mind-set that is required for looking at the world and constantly trying to discern the current context around relevant issues and how they may affect the organization in the future. It's worthwhile to cultivate that mind-set. Being a turnaround specialist does not mean that I ever want to do it again. As extraordinary as those days were in many ways, no one in the system wants to relive them.

CHAPTER THREE

Use Quality to Achieve High Performance: The Baldrige Framework

The thing is to keep everything in motion and take the work to the man and not the man to the work.

—Henry Ford

On November 21, 2011, I got a call at home to say that Henry Ford Health System had won the Malcolm Baldrige National Quality Award. Winning such a noted prize was the proudest moment in my career, and it was made even better because it was my birthday. But it had been a difficult couple of weeks. My partner, Pam, had lost her mom the day before, after several long weeks taking care of her in our home. We had her family staying with us as well, and people were coming and going.

I knew the Baldrige call was coming; I just didn't know if we had won. If we lost, I was told, we would receive word from a gentleman who was charged with reaching out to the runners-up. If we won, the deputy secretary of commerce, who was a woman, would call with the good news. When the phone finally rang, I saw the Washington, DC, area code and I froze for a second. Pam was standing in the doorway with a questioning expression, one thumb up in the air—she wanted to know if we got it. I remember picking up the phone, saying hello and hearing a woman's voice on the other end. After that I don't really remember what she said—but I knew we had won and it was pretty thrilling.

The news was exciting, not only for me but for the entire health system. It was an incredible validation of the work we had accomplished and the vision we had for the organization. But winning at a time when Pam was losing her mom poignantly underscored, for me, the importance of quality in health care and the amazing difference it can make in people's lives, and even at the end of life.

"Quality" sums up pretty much everything I have tried to do at HFHS, and all that Gail Warden did before me. In fact, HFHS began working on quality improvement twenty years ago when Gail and former senior vice president Vinod Sahney first brought total quality management into the system. Gail and Vin were pioneers in the healthcare quality movement and two of the founding board members for the Institute for Healthcare Improvement, which was incorporated in Michigan. Vin was the person who first introduced me to Baldrige when I was working in Akron, and I was hooked.

The bottom line, in health care, is that quality is an expectation of clinical performance. That's the main reason I started us on the Baldrige journey—and it was rigorous and incredible from start to finish. The application process is a challenge unto itself, and that's where most companies halt the effort. But the challenge involved more than just the logistical resources required—the initiative forced us to identify our priorities and focus on them. Over the seven years that we participated, we received continuous feedback from the Baldrige examiners and we kept getting better and better as a result. The effort had a cumulative effect with every attempt. Our metrics improved, our system integration got better, and our service was enhanced. Not many organizations have the patience and perseverance to apply year after year, but I was convinced this could be an important ingredient in our success.

Between 2004 and 2011, we spent two years learning the Baldrige framework and preparing to apply, and we applied for five consecutive years. If you think about Michigan at that time, it was a very rough environment. We began to see the auto industry slipping into decline, the nation went through the great recession, and Detroit was experiencing a population slide that decimated the city. Even so, HFHS managed to win the Baldrige equivalent quality award at the state level in 2007. That fueled our desire to win nationally. But there were plenty of people who felt we had too much on our plate already. We were continually faced with potentially competing priorities. The Baldrige was a challenge every year, particularly when we were building a new hospital and acquiring two others. I had people say to me, "Nancy, we should just take a year off. We have other things to do." I just said *no*, because I knew that if we paused we would lose momentum and our focus on performance improvement would diminish.

Over the years, internal support for winning the award snowballed. We even had more than twenty-five people in the organization volunteer for the laborious training needed to become a Baldrige examiner. They were fully engaged in the program and it gave me a lot of support. These folks did not want to see us falter or give up—and their determination was contagious. During our site visit in 2011, a team of examiners came for a week and met with 1,200 of our employees. They looked at our leadership systems, clinical results, and financials—and every aspect of the organization. We needed all 23,000 employees to be on the same page and you just can't fake that.

I remember talking to a security guard after we announced that we had won. He told me he was the first person who greeted the Baldrige examiners when they arrived. I asked what he told them and he said: "I said that every day I try to do the very best job that I can for our staff and patients." I said, "Well, then you've won the Baldrige award for us, because you obviously created an amazing first impression."

It felt the same all across the organization. Every single person had won the award. It was an iconic moment for us. At the time, we were the largest, most complicated, most academic organization in health care to ever win the designation. The entire system benefited in a number of ways that we inculcated into the corporate culture over that seven-year period and every year since.

What I learned from Henry Ford about quality is that without it everything else crumbles. Because of that tendency, quality and ongoing improvement needed to be hard-wired into the culture—just as Henry Ford promoted quality by making assembly line manufacturing a centerpiece at Ford Motor Company. This culture of continuous improvement helped the organization control quality as well as cost. At HFHS, the cultural underpinnings that we developed during our Baldrige journey enabled us to build a culture that strives for quality. I will offer some details about how and why we won because I believe they may be instructive. The fact is that the Baldrige model served our needs extremely well, motivating us to improve performance and instill quality across the organization.

A Framework for Improvement

Most people apply for the Baldrige with the obvious goal in mind—to win the prize. It's a badge of honor that bestows prestige and serves as a seal of approval. Regardless of the associated glow for the recipient, very few companies apply as many times as we did. Again, the need for a carefully conceived, well-organized fifty-page application puts most people off. It reminds me of what Bill Ford from the Ford Motor Company said when introducing me at an event in Michigan: "You know, at Ford Motor Company we didn't do all that well in filling out the application, let alone winning." He was making a joke, of course, but his message was that simply making your way through the process is a challenge.

And that was precisely the point for us. The process of participating requires the same level of coordination and involvement that the award is designed to recognize. We spent two years learning about Baldrige and five years applying—because we were using the process as a mechanism for change. This push was happening just after the turnaround, so people saw the activity as an organic part of our performance improvement effort. In fact, over the course of five years we didn't use the word "Baldrige" much around the organization. We borrowed the framework as a structure for operating, but we didn't talk about the award. We were so focused on improvement that when the Baldrige site visit was at hand, in 2011, people were scratching their heads and saying, "Well, what's Baldrige?" We had to do some quick educating!

For me, the rationale behind applying was twofold. First, I wanted the system to continue to get better. Baldrige judges an organization based on every aspect of its business and operations, and I felt the exercise would give us a solid framework for improvement. Second, the application process would force us to think deeply about efficiency. Designed to improve processes, Baldrige looks for consistency and minimal variation throughout all elements of the operation. This was especially appealing to me because I knew we needed to further integrate our offerings. With that in mind, we decided to apply as a system. It would have been far easier to win if we had applied as a single hospital or business unit, but I wanted Henry Ford to operate in concert. Going after the most challenging prize, then, held the greatest upside.

There are a number of things that chasing the Baldrige brought to us, and in many ways they, along with a culture of innovation, are what define us and continue to sustain us as an organization. What these elements add up to is quality, which we can look at in a number of cross-sections, including efficiency, safety, and performance.

1. Efficiency

Fragmented, high-cost service delivery has been a well-documented failing of U.S. health care. That said, HFHS has always tried to set a high standard in this area because efficiency resides in our DNA. Henry Ford wanted to create products that would advance the country, and he wanted to do it through work processes that were very efficient. For example, when Henry Ford Hospital first opened its doors in 1915, it integrated inpatient and outpatient departments under one management structure. Further, as the hospital grew into a system, it continued to pioneer models to integrate care and delivery. We were early adopters of electronic medical records (EMR), an essential tool for coordinating care. And we integrated financing and delivery by adding a health insurance plan created to deliver low-cost and high-quality care.

Many other examples stand out, but efficiency is an ongoing challenge. For instance, after the turnaround took hold we wanted to bring the expanding health system together in a way that would notably raise the bar for service and performance. In this case, integration meant ensuring that all patients who sought care at any Henry Ford facility would receive the same level of high-quality attention. The Baldrige criteria helped us attack this in a strategic way. The objective was to standardize care protocols across the system and develop a culture of performance excellence among more than thirty thousand employees, physicians, and volunteers.

Delivering on that goal required merging a number of hospital functions. Pathology offers one example: until 2007, each facility had its own laboratory services and private pathology group. According to Dr. Richard Zarbo, senior vice president for pathology and laboratory medicine, "There was no means of standardizing across the system to ensure that all patients saw the same reference ranges, for instance, or even had the same quality on a pathology report."[1]

This was extraordinarily frustrating for Dr. Zarbo, who was chair of the College of American Pathologists Quality Committee, and it was disconcerting for doctors and patients alike. Under Dr. Zarbo's leadership, the disparate lab services were eventually integrated. Practically speaking, that meant around-the-clock results were available throughout the system—previously, some of the suburban hospitals had more limited hours and communication protocols.

Another important target of integration involved strengthening the relationship between the system's internal medical group and its many independent practice physicians. In 2010, we created the Henry Ford Physician Network as a way to remove barriers to patient care coordination across providers. Run by physicians, the network encouraged collaboration and standardized a higher quality of care while lowering costs. Despite the potential benefits of the network, it was nonetheless a tough sell to independent physicians operating within HFHS who wanted to maintain their autonomy. After much debate, the network was formed to include all Henry Ford Medical Group physicians and also those in independent practice who elect to belong—a total of 1,900 physicians in 2015.

It was around this time that the system's nurses also created a mechanism for sharing solutions and standardizing best practices. Connie Cronin, former chief nursing officer for the system, said, "It's important that you have your own identity, but you have to work together. There needs to be similarities across the system, otherwise you are not a system...you're just a group of places." Connie recognized an opportunity to bring nursing leadership from across HFHS together to accomplish common goals. Topping the agenda were quality and safety standards. The Corporate Nurse Executive Council, now under the leadership of CNO Veronica Hall, meets monthly to standardize clinical protocols, policies, procedures, and even job descriptions.[2]

Business planning, as well, became much more integrated during the Baldrige process and ever since. William Schramm, senior vice president of business development, says that a lot of the work by his group does not necessarily concern mergers or acquisitions, but is more about creating synergy through collaborative planning and program development. In essence, he said, his group is helping the organization to achieve a desired business model, which is a compilation of the products and services in our portfolio. He summed it up this way: "How do you leverage those products and services to sustain the enterprise over the long term? It really is looking inside and outside the organization to bring together the right pieces and the right approach to sustain the organization."[3]

The system's move to a more integrated model allowed HFHS patients to proceed more seamlessly across sites of care. Interestingly, one of the things that integration accelerated was expansion. We wanted patients to have better geographic access in every part of the market. Our Detroit hospital is centrally located and we had another hospital in the southern part of our primary region, but we did not have any major hospitals to the north at the time. So the launch of two new HFHS hospitals, one that was acquired and another we built, allowed us to improve coverage measurably. In addition, we built ambulatory networks around each in order to enhance our competitive position and strengthen access for patients in need.

Integration has always been a key ingredient to our success, but it was radically accelerated as part of the Baldrige framework we embraced after the turnaround work was completed.

2. Safety

Henry Ford created a cadre of safety procedures that dramatically reduced injury rates for workers at Ford Motor Company—including assigning individuals to a specific location instead of allowing them to roam all about. These were remarkably innovative measures at the time. In his autobiography, Ford mentions the safety benefits of an assembly line, including the fact that workers didn't engage in heavy lifting, sudden stopping, or repeated bending.[4] In a health-care setting, quality is all about safety. That involves patient safety, first and foremost, but also includes safety for the doctors, nurses, and staff members. Safety is what makes and breaks reputations in health care. Without it, liability becomes an issue and fundamentals such as service, trust, ethical conduct, and reliability all vanish.

Patient safety can be measured in "harm events"—including infections, surgical complications, adverse drug interactions, and misdiagnoses—and by examining mortality rates. In terms of the Baldrige, there was a positive symmetry at play: our work around safety was a leading reason we won the award, and the Baldrige process itself was the main tool we used to focus on improving our safety record.

One area in which we set a new standard in safety was depression care. Most hospitals at the time created metrics around reducing a patient's symptoms or severity of depression, but we wanted to go further faster. We started by targeting an audacious goal originally proposed by a nurse at HFHS—perfect depression care. To us, truly effective depression care meant that no patients under our care would die from suicide—and we set out to make that happen. In the first four years of the program, the suicide rate among patients fell by 75 percent. Then, in year five, we achieved our goal of eliminating suicides among our patients and have maintained that ideal for more than a decade.[5]

Our successes in depression care dovetailed nicely with an Institute for Healthcare Improvement initiative called the "100,000 Lives Campaign." Introduced in 2005, the initiative was geared toward dramatically reducing morbidity and mortality linked to treatment-related infections nationwide over an eighteen-month period. HFHS contributed to that by saving two hundred lives. Out of that came our own evidence-based "No Harm Campaign," a system-wide sharing of best clinical practices aimed at reducing or eliminating twenty-three sources of harm. Led by Dr. William Conway, then the system's chief quality officer, the campaign resulted in a 26 percent reduction in harm events between 2008 and 2011, when most hospitals' rates of reduction were in the single digits.

According to the Institute for Healthcare Improvement, this program is a national best practice. One prime example of this success was Henry Ford Hospital's reduction in central-line infections from ten per year in 2008 to three in 2011. HFHS has accomplished a 40 percent reduction in mortality since 2004—a result of successful implementation and spread of several improvements. In addition, our definition of harm in the campaign included all harm, whether preventable by standard practices or not. For example, when standard best practices to reduce catheter-related bloodstream infections in hemodialysis patients resulted in only modest improvements, our team developed entirely new best practices. The new system led to a 34 percent decrease in dialysis mortality since its implementation.[6] Holding ourselves accountable for patient safety motivated us to find ways to overcome difficult challenges to meet goals.

The work we did during the turnaround, and the focused efforts to dramatically improve quality using the Baldrige framework, enabled us to develop a culture of safety that has, I believe, been crucial to our success.

3. Performance

The Baldrige criteria are about performance excellence—achieved through aligned and integrated processes. While it's certainly a bigger challenge to deploy these processes across all parts of a large organization such as Henry Ford, the underlying principles, and the commensurate improvements, are intended to be the same for any company. As noted, we started our journey with the intention of using the framework to become better—not simply to win an award. Using that thinking, we integrated the Baldrige criteria into our strategic planning and business operations, and it became part of our routine.

The Baldrige Criteria

- Growth in customer satisfaction, engagement, and loyalty
- World-class product and service outcomes
- Role model process efficiency
- Increased workforce satisfaction and engagement
- Growth in revenue and market share, and improved financial results
- Increased learning outcomes
- Improved outcomes (safety and loyalty)

Health care is not a level playing field. For us, pure financial performance is a little different than it is for a public company, or even many other hospitals, because we have so much uncompensated care. If you applied our performance from a cost and revenue standpoint to other markets, even in southeast Michigan, we'd be making a lot more money. Even so, the Baldrige criteria added a strict discipline to the way we plan, execute, and evaluate our performance. Just as Bill Conway and I said when we received the award, our organization took a "zero-defect, no-excuses" approach to health care. The use of dashboards and benchmarking (and comparisons to companies outside the health-care arena) allowed us to measure performance in a manner that pointed us toward top performance. We use the Baldrige criteria to assess key investments, update management systems, and set system priorities. They are also the foundation for our seven-pillar framework, and are reflected in the competencies that drive leadership development and personnel evaluations.

---

7 Pillars of Performance

I created the "7 Pillars of Performance" at Henry Ford to keep us tethered to the fundamental areas that drive excellence for us. Although they predate our Baldrige journey, during the time we competed for the Baldrige, the pillars became the core construct we use within business units to measure success. As such, they strengthen integration and bring the system closer together.

1. People
2. Quality and safety
3. Service
4. Growth
5. Community
6. Research and education
7. Finance

The first three pillars—people, quality and safety, and service— are core because they dictate and drive the rest. The people pillar is first, very intentionally, because I believe that if you fail to engage individuals within the organization everything else falters. The quality and safety pillar, as well, is central to all our efforts. As I mentioned, we have been on a quality journey for more than twenty years, and our safety programs have become a benchmark in the industry. The next pillar, service, centers on the patient experience and fans out to include families as well as our own caregivers, such as physicians and nurses. As you might imagine, service is inextricably tied to people and quality and safety.

Growth, although arguably a result of good performance, is the pillar that keeps us facing forward. In health care, I have found, people sometimes consider growth to be a benefit rather than a strategic focus. Patients show up in the ER and we serve them—end of story. But a hospital, like any other business, needs to create marketing strategies and brand objectives, and to understand the needs of customers.

The next two pillars—community and research and education— are likewise a less common focus for most health systems. As an anchor institution of Detroit, however, we were founded to serve the community and, in essence, we are a neighborhood asset. As such, we connect to the community through a variety of outreach initiatives and strive to create collaborative partnerships, stepping up when the community needs our support. Academics has also been a part of our core since our creation, when Henry Ford made it his mission to bring the best doctors over from Johns Hopkins University, and ten years later, when Clara Ford decided to found a nursing school.

We built a pillar around education and research to keep us focused on the requisite opportunities and threats that come with being an academic institution. For instance, an academic program attracts remarkable talent because the brightest people in the field often want to teach, innovate, and advance the science and art of medicine, nursing, and allied health professions. In terms of looming threats, we rely heavily on graduate medical education payments from the federal and state government, so we must constantly be ready for changes in payment policies and legislation.

The final pillar is finance. We put it last, intentionally, because if the other six pillars are strong, we believe we will have a stable financial organization. Yet, the finance pillar is where a lot of our performance monitoring and management support are provided; through a project management office, our leaders can access the analytics, support, and technology that help them make good business decisions.

While the seven-pillar structure aids the integration of the business units, emphasizing that they are part of a larger system, it also leaves directors free to manage their units with an appropriate amount of autonomy. The pillars provide the desired "ends"—but creative, innovative leaders and caregivers have the freedom to determine the "means" by which they will achieve the results.

The Baldrige criteria propelled us to "think big," even beyond the seven pillars, and to compare our organization with top companies across the country. That mode of thinking and operating was rather new for HFHS. When I came to Henry Ford, there was a deeply embedded belief that suburban patients would never come downtown for care. Employees believed there was a limit to how well we could perform and grow, financially and otherwise. The thinking was, "Well, this is the inner city. If we have a dreary hospital that's not clean and we have low patient satisfaction and employee morale, what do you expect? This is as good as it gets in Detroit." That was unacceptable to me.

As part of our culture work, we tried to eliminate the victim mentality. We also tried to expunge the belief that we couldn't attract patients from a broader geography. The turning point came down to one major win—the Vattikuti Urology Institute's robotic surgery program. The minute Dr. Menon started bringing patients in from outside the U.S. (and domestically from all fifty states), the context changed for us. We learned that we could attract patients from anywhere if we had world-class programs and superb service.

The other idea I reshaped to point performance upward was the context around our market size. I had worked in much smaller markets, and we had always been able to attract new patients. We had a 4.5 million-person population base in Detroit. We didn't have to attract all of them, but we certainly could attract many more than we were. It was all about maintaining a positive mind-set. I was a relentless cheerleader for Detroit and for Henry Ford, and I never accepted negativity.

Our Baldrige work gave us the structure to push past our self-limiting mind-set. In fact, a number of the major strategic moves that we made between 2007 and 2011 were influenced by our Baldrige journey. The two new hospitals and our ambulatory centers, for example, signaled significant expansion and required careful planning and teamwork. I believed at the time, as I do now, that Baldrige enhanced our ability to accomplish those projects because we were thinking differently about process, organization, leadership, timelines, and budgets.

Not only did the Baldrige structure help drive growth, it also helped us to fund it. It was the consistency of our improved performance over a period of several years that enabled us to issue debt to pay for some of those capital projects. Furthermore, it gave confidence to philanthropic donors, contributing to our growth and helping us to raise $270 million in our capital campaign over a period of about seven years.

Finally, I would posit that our Baldrige journey opened the door for direct net gains, thanks to reduced costs. That would seem self-evident in most industries—improving the quality of a system can reduce costs—but it was not always the case in health care. Why? Insurers and Medicare at the time were paying hospitals for the higher utilization generated by mistakes, errors, or bad outcomes.[7] In essence, the medical system had built-in financial incentives for bad care.[8] Then, when

Medicare changed its rules in 2007, hospitals were held accountable for certain common errors. By improving care and eliminating patient harm events, Henry Ford Hospital reduced expenses by $1.9 million, or $40 per patient, in 2010. We extrapolated the cost savings over our five hospitals to the tune of $10 million. As Bill Conway has said, "You can save lives and save dollars at the same time."

The Next Journey

Quality is what moved the needle for HFHS in terms of improvement—through safety, efficiency, and an overall elevated performance. We got better by leaps and bounds during our Baldrige journey, and one common overlay was innovation, which I will address in chapter 4. Suffice it to say that ongoing improvement through radical moves is enabled from the top. Leaders need to empower everyone within the organization and instill a sense of urgency. More than just "saying yes" to ideas or sponsoring programs, I was orchestrating the efforts, and senior leaders across HFHS were fully involved as well, so the entire system was engaged in the pursuit of improving quality. This included our Board of Trustees, which, in 2007, made patient safety their top priority for the system.

In the end, we got what we hoped for from the Baldrige journey. And we've continued to improve ever since. That translates into better financial performance, growth, higher levels of patient engagement, and lower employee turnover. In addition to the legacy of improvement, we also gained confidence. Just as athletes and musicians need confidence to perform, so, too, do people trying to accomplish great things within an organization.

When I am asked if I believed we would win the Baldrige, I usually just smile. We weren't exactly "in it to win it" at first—although I would never have said that when we were doing double time working on the applications. But there was a tipping point. We gained traction, and the competitive energy of the organization took on a life of its own. We grew more and more engaged, expert, and confident, which served us well. Because we were in Detroit as the auto industry imploded and the city declared bankruptcy, the fact that we won the Baldrige against all odds instilled within us a sense that we could move forward and do great things despite the seemingly intractable problems that surrounded us.

The final word on quality and improvement is that the work itself is never complete. The goalpost is forever shifting. At HFHS, we've added a new clinical information system and a revenue cycle across the whole system that essentially embeds the quality work into our day-to-day efforts of caregivers and support staff. We also have a new chief quality officer whose mission it is to move us to the next level. As a part of that effort, we plan to improve our metrics dramatically. The airline and nuclear power industries have done just that, but health care has yet to get there. We are working to be out in front. Our new president, Wright L. Lassiter III, will lead us in that effort, much like my predecessor brought us to quality improvement in health care and I took us though the Baldrige journey. Wright, who is my successor, is going to be the leader who will move us to the high level of reliability that we seek to attain.

Succession is inevitable. Despite the inescapable changes that will come, we need to have foundational principles and values that remain constant even as the people and events around us evolve. We will look at some of those bedrock ideas in the next chapter and explore how they instill a desire to innovate.

CHAPTER FOUR

Find the Disrupters in Your Organization—and Listen to Them

Our invariable reply to "It can't be done" is "Go do it."

—Henry Ford[1]

Most people have an image in their mind about what a hospital should look like. It's the iconic snapshot of a large, sterile institution with white walls and large, paneled elevators that go up into the sky. The gift shop in the lobby sells balloons, flowers, candy, magazines, pajamas, and a few gift items. The adjacent cafeteria serves pizza, burgers, soup, and sandwiches, and there's a separate coffee shop or newspaper stand with additional drinks and menu items. End of story. People aren't searching out hospitals for their world-class cuisine or shopping—they come for medical care and they come to get well. Right?

It's interesting to see how people react when you disrupt their core beliefs about something, like a hospital, that is seen as a public resource. Some people roll with it, while others are less accepting. Every person has a different tolerance for change, and mine happens to be fairly high, so I have always been a proponent of taking risks on innovation.

In 2009, we opened the system's first new hospital since 1915. We had acquired hospitals previously, but this one, in West Bloomfield, Michigan, was the only one we conceived and built from the foundation up. Deciding to build the hospital was a historic moment for us, and I saw it as an opportunity to create the hospital of the future. Still, it was a major undertaking at a time when many organizations were retrenching.

At that time, Michigan had the highest unemployment rate of any state in the U.S. and the entire nation was reeling from the great recession and the subprime mortgage crisis that preceded it. As for Detroit, all of the economic indicators were negative: home prices were declining and poverty was rising. For me, the situation brought to mind the state of Henry Ford Hospital several years earlier, before we turned the tide. Employee morale had become a problem and the building looked like it was falling down around us. But once we were able to invest in infrastructure and attend to aesthetics and services at the hospital, moods began to improve—and so did our performance. The other thing that lifted us back up was the groundbreaking robotic surgery techniques at the Vattikuti Urology Institute. As mentioned, they altered our DNA: suddenly we were at the cutting edge, with state-of-the-art credibility to uphold.

Fast-forward a few years to our blueprints for West Bloomfield. Given the market and our own budget constraints, it might have been easier (and some would say wiser) to build a traditional hospital without high-end amenities. Families everywhere were doing more with less, the thinking went, and we should do the same. That was one school of thought—but it didn't happen that way, thanks in large part to the man I hired to run the new hospital. Instead, we built a "health and wellness center" that was equipped with eateries that offered gourmet cuisine, a beautiful day spa, a greenhouse and indoor farmer's market, a demonstration kitchen, and a retail atrium filled with live plants and curved paths edged in cobblestone.

It was a hospital that had the look and feel of a luxury hotel, right down to the trendy retailers, tea sommelier, and concierge. Young couples have had their wedding receptions at this hospital, that's how beautiful it is.

The visionary disruptor who was my partner in creating the $360 million facility was Gerard van Grinsven, a longtime Ritz-Carlton executive who had opened twenty properties around the world, served as VP of food and beverage, and led a turnaround of the Ritz-Carlton in Dearborn, Michigan. Gerard knew his way around a five-star hotel, but he had no hospital experience whatsoever. Still, when he met with me for coffee at my home and asked for career advice, I recognized an opportunity. He had a strong vision that coincided with my own and a reputation as an excellent leader. I hired him on the spot and decided that he could fill the high-stakes position as CEO of our new hospital. It was an unorthodox choice and there was some apprehension internally at HFHS. The wider industry, as well, was alight with disdain. Yet, based on Gerard's unique experience, I believed that Henry Ford would approve of my choice of leaders. Ford's attitude was this: "It is not easy to get away from tradition. That is why all our new operations are always directed by men who have had no previous knowledge of the subject and therefore have not had a chance to get on really familiar terms with the impossible."[2] Thanks to Gerard's distinctive background, he was able to help us escape from tradition. Together, with other leaders at the organization, we changed minds and forged ahead.

Although complicated to execute and initially somewhat unpopular externally, the maneuver was extremely innovative—and in the end the project managed to succeed beyond anyone's expectations. It turns out that people quite like coming to a place that doesn't remind them of a hospital, and will even change their doctor to be able to do so![3]

This type of breakthrough thinking, from Gerard and many others, is the reason I got into health care initially. My memories of hospitals growing up were grim, and I knew we could make the experience far better and perhaps set a new standard for the industry—not only in terms of aesthetics but also standard of care. Gerard would argue, and

I concur, that West Bloomfield represents a way of rethinking the role of a hospital. In positioning ourselves as a community center for well-being, we created a destination that helps people lead healthier lives.

West Bloomfield was a game changer for us, and it was one of the things that opened the floodgates. A century or more after Henry Ford revolutionized auto manufacturing, we at HFHS have leveraged his legacy to introduce new ideas and concepts designed to shake up both our own thinking and the world of health care. Innovation has always been one of our greatest strengths, dating back to our founder, and we started to wield it more effectively than ever before. When we went through the Baldrige application process we identified what we thought were our core competencies: care coordination, collaboration, and innovation. Innovation has been in our makeup from the beginning, but we needed to nurture it.

Innovation in Health Care

West Bloomfield created a stir, in part because health care is behind the curve when it comes to innovation. While the medical field has made immense strides—with treatments, drug therapies, and medical devices—health care is stuck in the dark ages in terms of financing and delivery. Similarly, while there is much to say about advances in brain research and gene sequencing, little or nothing radical comes to mind when we look at business models. The Affordable Care Act and its antecedents may eventually change the game, but for the moment we are stuck in a holding pattern, with expensive treatments and a fragmented and largely inefficient industry.

There are a number of reasons for this. First, if you look at how most health-care organizations are structured you'll seldom see a truly robust R&D department, whereas the pharmaceutical and biotechnology industries have R&D carved right into their business models. Next, although parts of health care are well funded, the industry is complex and its largest interest groups remain at odds with one another. They seldom work together in the direction of progress. Finally, government regulation and legislation, although necessary, slow innovation and distract the industry from becoming more effective and responsive to consumer needs.

These are all major forces, and I can't say that HFHS has the silver-bullet solution. However, what I can say is that HFHS is a case study in making innovation a priority. It is a noted part of our culture, first, because our legacy dates back to an innovator, Henry Ford himself, and second, because we've needed to be creative in order to survive in Detroit. In fact, creativity and our commitment to the surrounding community are the two reasons we are still here. The leaders who preceded me—Dr. Robin Buerki, beginning in the 1950s; Stanley Nelson, from 1971 to 1990; and my predecessor Gail Warden—each traveled different but deliberate paths toward innovation. And that's part of the reason I came to HFHS. Innovation is our secret sauce.

For me, a passion for progress began early, thanks to my father. Like most teenagers, I had no clue what my parents did for a living. Then, when I was in college, I worked as a summer intern at my dad's company. I talked with people and immediately saw how much people respected him. I was astounded to learn that he was responsible for two of the most important components the company had invented. All I could say was, "Really?" His patents were related to nuclear parts made for steam generators, so this was high-end stuff. But more than anything else, he considered himself a problem solver. He was a tinkerer who never gave up. I saw that in him every day and I admired it. I also internalized it, and when I settled into my own career I felt an overwhelming desire to make things better.

At HFHS, during his tenure as CEO, Gail Warden launched a number of important health services research centers that remain central to what we do today—and our focus on basic science and applied research has only accelerated. In fact, we receive about $70 million in annual funding for research from internal and outside sources, putting us in the top 20 percent of all institutions granted funding by the NIH and U.S. Public Health Service, and first in Michigan for NIH-research funding for non-university-based health care systems.

Part of my contribution to accelerating innovative solutions has been to focus us beyond academia and to better integrate our R&D activities into our daily operations. Most people think "operations" is about managing the status quo but I've never looked at it that way. To me, operations occurs at the hospital level, where people are running the business—in the clinics and outpatient centers and even in our retail and insurance operations. My goal has been to enable and encourage innovation and make sure it's applied and integrated at all levels for the greatest impact.

For example, General Motors contacted us several years ago about instituting a system of e-prescribing for all HFHS physicians. E-prescriptions, or electronic prescriptions, take the place of paper and fax prescriptions, and increase the use of cost-effective generic medications while decreasing complications from medication incompatibility. Prescribing electronically also represents a more customer-friendly approach to getting medications. Given the obvious benefits, one would think that transition to such a system would be simple—but change management around this and other innovations has been difficult across the industry. When GM first approached us our IT people said, "No, we're just not equipped to do that." Part of the problem was the challenge of spreading this new technology not only with our system doctors but also with physicians in other HAP networks. But Fran Parker, the CEO of our health plan at the time, and I pushed. We told GM: "Yes, we absolutely can," and I asked the medical group and HAP to work together to make it happen. Getting 1,200 doctors in the medical group on board with e-prescribing within one year was the first step and one of the fastest change processes any of us had ever seen.

In addition to being an innovation enabler, I am a champion of the disrupters within our organization. I seek them out and listen to their ideas and aspirations. And there are a lot of disrupters. Once people see that I identify with innovators and iconoclasts, they come out of hiding with their plans and ideas. When pressure to deliver quality care to a growing population meets tight schedules and finite resources, HFHS employees—from the cafeteria to the operating rooms—find ways to innovate and disrupt old ways of working. They offer smart, quick solutions to everyday problems as well as big, bold new ideas for devices and technologies. I will talk about some of those amazing things first, and then describe how we have been able to listen to the disrupters and make innovation one of our core competencies.

A Few Cool Things

If you scan our media coverage over time and look at how we're drawing in patients, you'll see that it's due to innovation. The approach we used in designing West Bloomfield Hospital is one innovation, but there are many more—everything from pioneering clinical services to breakthrough ideas that have captured wide attention. As I mentioned, innovation is what has driven our growth and financial success, and it gave us back our momentum at a critical time. It has put us on the map in ways too numerous to mention, but I will hit on some of my favorite advancements, to show some of the things we have accomplished in the past fifteen years.

Minimally invasive surgery. It always seems to come back to this one for me. Dr. Mani Menon's work did more than make Henry Ford Hospital feel special again; it also created a new foundation for clinical excellence. As part of Dr. Menon's work, Henry Ford Medical Group physicians performed the first robotic removal of a cancerous prostate gland in the U.S. using a special nerve-sparing technique—an innovation that revolutionized prostate cancer treatment globally. Today, five surgical specialties have expanded into the robotics field, and the Medical Group is recognized for its widespread expertise in minimally invasive surgery.

3-D printing treatments. Each person's heart and heart valves are unique; therefore, prosthetic valves may fit imperfectly, leak, or interfere with other heart structures. Our Structural Heart Team[4] at Henry Ford Hospital, under the leadership of Dr. Bill O'Neill, uses 3-D printing to create exact replicas of individual human hearts in order to precisely size and plan valve replacements. The team can look at what they had planned for that procedure and modify it in near real time. Never before could a physician examine an exact replica of a patient's body part, with her hands outside a patient's body and without ever making an incision. This innovation brings personalized medicine to the forefront of patient-centered care.

Tools and devices. One frontline nurse recently worked with our Innovation Institute to develop a handy tool for opening the heavy metal containers, called Genesis containers, that hold sterilized surgical instruments. These Genesis containers must be pried apart after flipping open tight, spring-based metal tabs. Nurses in the operating room need to open dozens of these metal boxes every day, causing carpal tunnel syndrome and other serious injuries. The innovative pop-top "can opener" the team created to unseal containers is so incredibly useful that we sent one to every operating room nurse across our system on Nurse's Day in 2015.

Process improvement. Our chair of pathology, Dr. Richard Zarbo, came to me and the system's medical leaders with a plan to transform our labs using Six Sigma and lean management approaches. His idea was to roll out what he called the Henry Ford Production Model. The improvements have resulted in quality and process updates that include reduced overlap, process automation, and shorter timelines as well as standardized equipment and reduced human error. In short, they have yielded some extraordinary process advances. Today, Dr. Zarbo teaches these techniques in labs across the country, and he trains teams at HFHS and beyond to improve process and drive better outcomes of care. It's been a great success story.

Patient gowns. We received considerable national media attention for a simple and smart innovation that enhanced patient satisfaction enormously—an improved hospital gown. The new gown was the first to address one of the most common style complaints from patients—namely that the open back of the gown is drafty, embarrassing, and uncomfortable. About the improved design, comedian Ellen DeGeneres smartly quipped: "Leave it to Ford to cover the *junk* in your *trunk*."

New delivery models. Cognizant that younger generations want a speedier, more convenient outpatient health-care delivery experience, HFHS pioneered a new kind of clinic, called QuickCare, in Downtown Detroit. Staffed with Henry Ford Hospital nurse practitioners, in consultation with physicians, as needed, QuickCare offers what we are calling Radical Convenience—an on-demand approach to medical care that will help us meet increased demand following the passage of the Affordable Care Act. In addition to routine primary and urgent care, services include acupuncture, massage, and immunizations for traveling abroad.

The Innovation Institute

Academic institutions are structured to deliver education. Health-care organizations are designed to deliver quality health care to patients. Neither of these functional areas is set up to support an innovation team tasked with commercializing opportunities and creating new businesses. But because of our mandate and mission, we have made a strong commitment to commercial innovation as something that's of clear institutional value. As a result, we created the Innovation Institute as a separate entity, with funding to support professional innovators and designers.

Launched in 2012 under the leadership of Dr. Scott A. Dulchavsky, chairman of surgery at Henry Ford Hospital, the Innovation Institute is a way to codify the system's inventive culture and create a mechanism for commercializing the innovative ideas that come from staff and practitioners. The institute focuses on engineering innovative solutions to problems and shaping the future of health care. Both a physical and virtual resource, it provides system innovators with access to resources and programs including opportunity assessment, engineering services for prototypes, seminars designed to convey opportunities, programs aimed at developing specific medical products, and educational offerings in areas such as translational medicine and the entrepreneurial arts. The disciplined process has oversight from Dr. Dulchavsky but also from our chief innovation officer, Mark Coticchia, thereby joining clinical and business expertise.

Housed in a retooled 1924 Albert Kahn building at the center of the Henry Ford Hospital complex, the institute's seventeen employees—including designers from the Detroit College for Creative Studies—work on high-tech tools for robotic surgery and on software for applications such as fitness tracking, as well as on solving thorny problems like lowering readmission rates for patients once they leave the hospital. We now have more than three hundred projects sourced from all parts of the health system being funded through philanthropic and industry support.

The institute partners with private-sector companies as well. Institute leaders have created a robust corporate innovation program that invites companies from medical device firms to small manufacturers to come to us with their ideas. What we bring is a multidisciplinary theme and an open innovation model. Recognizing that one of our biggest roadblocks to innovation is shaking ideas free from Henry Ford employees, as well as outside industry, the institute sponsors ongoing "innovation challenges" to draw out new solutions to some of health care's biggest unsolved problems.

Creating a Culture of Innovation

Barriers to innovation are everywhere in large organizations. People are busy and plowing ahead at full capacity, funding is targeted, and innovation is risky. When a person approaches a leader with an idea, he often gets shut down or turned away. There is always other complex work going on, so there's a tendency to say, "Let's get back to that idea later." But later never comes. Once leaders put up a wall, people back down. Another factor that blocks innovation is an organization's response to "failed" endeavors. How you respond to adversity either turns people off or keeps them coming back. To me, regardless of the outcome, innovation is always a learning opportunity and a building block.

Routing around these barriers and others requires a deep commitment. It would be simple to say that people have day jobs and innovation will happen as a matter of course. Some of us are natural-born entrepreneurs and others are not. But that thinking isn't enough to allow innovation to flourish, so I have tried to embed innovation deeper into our culture.

I am not the first leader at Henry Ford (starting foremost with our namesake) to put a stake in the ground and make innovation a priority. The culture work I put into place is a continuation of past efforts combined with new insights from our Baldrige journey. When we identified innovation as one of our core competencies, we needed to create clear pathways to enable it. The Innovation Institute, for one, has helped us to codify the way we innovate. And there are a number of other steps we took across the system to create an environment where people are constantly thinking about improvements and new ways of working. We have fostered the culture and given people permission to think differently in ways that make us stronger and able to thrive even when the environment around us is challenging.

Use a Problem-Solving Lens

One of the fundamental ways that we embed innovation into our culture is by putting a strong emphasis on creative problem solving. This perspective brings innovation right down to earth and has some important additional benefits.

First, associating innovation with problem solving allows us to focus squarely on the everyday task of serving patients better. It melds with our mission as caregivers and puts innovation front and center for everyone. For example, two Henry Ford doctors, frustrated with the outdated and inefficient pager-based system used for sharing information, developed StatChat—a communication tool that allows clinicians attending to a particular patient to see what other caregivers have done over the course of the patient's treatment.[5] Similarly, when doctors and nurses on the women's health team at Henry Ford found that new mothers were frequently overwhelmed by instructions delivered to them at discharge, they created a solution. They invented a system called Virtual Nurse, which uses avatar technology to help patients understand discharge information, allowing nurses to focus on areas where patients need more hands-on assistance. In both these cases, caregivers found a way to solve their own problem and better serve the needs of their patients.

Next, putting a problem-solving lens on innovation helps us zero in on solutions that are practical. A practical focus makes innovation urgent and accessible as opposed to esoteric. It also drives home the idea that anyone can invent and innovate. The new tool that helps operating room nurses open instrument containers is an excellent example. The device, conceived and prototyped in twenty-four hours, offers an immensely practical solution to an everyday problem that OR nurses had faced for years. Likewise, hospital gowns designed to provide better coverage have made thousands of patients happier and more comfortable in the hospital. It doesn't get much more practical than that.

Finally, problem solving keeps us focused on continual improvement. The "we can do better" mind-set, I have found, has prompted us to come up with genuine innovations. When there are no existing evidence-based ways to prevent a negative outcome, then innovators need to create a new approach in order to address it. We saw this over and over again as part of our "No Harm" campaign. For instance, when the conventional means to reduce catheter-related bloodstream infections in hemodialysis patients resulted in only modest improvements, we were motivated to develop a new best practice. The innovative "antibiotic lock protocol" we established has led to a 34 percent decrease in dialysis mortality since its implementation in 2008. In these cases and others, innovation equaled solving problems, plain and simple.

Keep It Inclusive

When I was head of strategic planning at Akron City Hospital I had a very small staff. There were three of us—not enough people to do the job the way that I wanted. I decided then and there that everyone across the organization was going to be a planner. Instead of trying to do everything with a few colleagues, I created a broader context for the organization so all employees could think differently about their work. My department provided a lot of data to management across the hospital, and we all became planners. Everyone was a part of the team.

That was one of the seeds of my philosophy on innovation. If there is one thing I firmly believe about innovation, it is that it can happen anywhere in an organization. It doesn't matter if you're a CEO, a housekeeper, a laundry worker, or a brain surgeon. Everyone, no matter their job description or pay grade, can and should be involved.

The benefits of an expansive perspective on innovation are numerous. The first is performance. When people are engaged in innovation they start to think big and they take ownership of their ideas and of the wider business. That ownership mind-set is empowering, and people get more involved in the success of their work, thereby pushing up performance. In addition, an organization of twenty-three thousand innovators can accomplish much more than one isolated group of professional designers who happen to be creative. At HFHS, anyone can bring an idea to our Innovation Institute, to his department head, or right to me. We get to look at more concepts that way and we talk to many more innovators about change and improvement. Lastly, a related upside of expansive innovation is engagement. Innovation is exciting and positive, and being a part of it makes everyone's job much more meaningful. And it is extremely useful for recruiting staff and physicians. If you were choosing between a vibrant workplace that puts a strong emphasis on cutting-edge ideas and one that is a little more traditional...well, let's just say that our spirit of innovation is a big draw for HFHS.

An additional benefit of thinking broadly about innovation, for us, has been getting beyond any one type of idea. A large number of innovators are bound to think about different aspects of our business: How do you improve process? How do you create new services? How do you look at clinical breakthroughs? And so on. These can be major innovations or smart incremental changes. Any doctor or employee can come in with a back-of-the-napkin idea. I look at it this way: you have to have a lot of base hits to win the pennant. With that mind-set, innovation can happen at any time, in any place, and with any person who is up at bat.

Incentivize Innovation

There are some innovations that don't cost much money. The tool that allows operating room nurses to access surgical instruments is a prime example: it's an extremely useful, low-tech device that is important but inexpensive to design and produce. I like those kinds of innovations, but not everything comes on the cheap. When we pursued Dr. Menon's robotic surgical solution, for example, we made the decision to invest in a cutting-edge operating room even as we were reducing costs pretty radically across the organization. Similarly, when we created the Innovation Institute we took $15 million out of our foundation to support the institute's setup and launch. When high-potential concepts present themselves, you need to pay attention.

No two innovations are alike. We pursue both mission-driven and commercially viable concepts. Mission-driven innovations aid us in our work as healers and are an important part of our responsibility as a teaching institution. Market-driven innovations, on the other hand, have commercial potential and, in theory, may offer a return on investment for the organization. Our award-winning hospital gown, for instance, is used not only in Henry Ford's five hospitals and thirty-two medical centers, but is licensed for use by other hospitals in the U.S. and abroad. Interestingly, that was a concept we expected to be primarily mission driven but that turned out to be a bona fide commercial opportunity. Regardless of the return, people at Henry Ford will tell you that if a notable idea bubbles up, there is usually a funding path to be discovered.

Another, more unconventional way that we invest in innovation is by incentivizing employees for being creative and injecting a little competition into the mix. The HFHS intellectual property policy offers innovators a 50 percent share of future revenues that come from product ideas that end up in the market. That's a pretty impressive call to action for employees who might have a great idea in their hip pocket. Our "Innovation Challenges" are even more of a major draw. These ongoing contests, run by the Innovation Institute, target specific problems and opportunities in health care by engineering the collision of talent and resources. For example, in 2015 the institute sponsored a competition that called on HFHS employees to submit their best ideas for clinical applications of wearable technology. Employees were not only encouraged but also incentivized to participate, with $10,000 in prizes offered. Finalists competed for an investment of seed capital and commercialization support.

Winning entries included:

- A system that used wearable activity trackers to record and encourage mobility of acute-care patients
- Wearable sensors used for total hip replacement patients that monitor and limit range of motion in rehab
- A health and wellness reminder system for elderly patients, leveraging location-based sensors and smart watches
- A mobile game interface, powered by activity trackers, designed to fight obesity by encouraging children to exercise

These challenges are very much in keeping with our Innovation Institute's mission. For years, we had a lot of good ideas that we pursued internally, but we seldom took the next step by commercializing them. We didn't have the bandwidth to translate them into business opportunities. The Innovation Institute takes these ideas and commercializes them, creating economic value for the hospital and the surrounding community—as well as for the innovators involved.

Yet, for me and for all of us here at HFHS, incentives for innovation are about more than splitting profits. Our Innovation Challenges are really about getting enthused to solve problems and keeping people engaged and satisfied by allowing them to be creative, no matter what their job description says.

Involve the Community

Health systems rely on their surrounding communities as much as the members of those communities depend on them for quality care. The relationship is reciprocal across the board—and innovation is no exception.

We want our organization to be part of the solution, to help figure out ways to make Detroit succeed because in doing so we succeed, and vice versa. Urban areas like Detroit are rich in diversity and creativity; as an anchor institution of the city, we've tapped into that richness to produce innovations that benefit both Henry Ford and Detroit residents in terms of economic value and state-of-the-art care.

Our vastly improved version of the hospital gown came about through a partnership we formed with the College for Creative Studies here in Detroit. I laugh when I think about how the idea emerged. We brought CCS students and faculty into the hospital to observe our work and they looked at the patients—walking around in the same gowns you'd find all across the world—and did a double take. They basically said, "You've got to be kidding me. You can't do any better than this?" They were right! It's no secret that patients in drafty hospital gowns feel uncomfortable and exposed.

So the CCS team went to work designing a gown that was warmer and more modest, and offered some basic features like a collar and a pocket. The designers met with doctors and nurses to understand what they needed in terms of access to the patients following a variety of procedures. Then we used Henry Ford Hospital as a learning laboratory to test the gowns, with numerous iterations of design. We knew that we were on to something when units within the hospital were competing to be the first to use them. Sometimes the greatest innovations are wonderfully simple.

It took a smart, objective, empathetic perspective, and help from the surrounding community, to see what we couldn't see. And that perspective works both ways. We've recently installed touch-screen health kiosks in churches and schools across Detroit. This bold initiative gives community residents the latest information about critical health issues such as diabetes, sexually transmitted infections, breast cancer, prenatal care, hypertension, and even alcoholism. Our objective is to disseminate important information to the people in Detroit by meeting them where they go. Many don't have Internet access where they live and they may visit the hospital only after it is too late—often in the end stage of a disease.

We developed the content in conjunction with local ministers and made the kiosks simple to operate—and they are getting tremendous use out in the community. Residents are better informed through more than seventy-five modules, community leaders are grateful, and our employees are proud. Contributing to the local community, and helping to improve it through innovation, is important not only to the community but also to the people who work within the system. They want to have an outlet, and formal programs, to not only commercialize great ideas but also to contribute to the local community from an economic development standpoint.

Keeping Innovation Alive

Henry Ford was an innovator, and that legacy puts innovation at the center of everything we do. We tend to be pretty laid back when an experiment doesn't pan out. After all, Ford wasn't successful every time. He was in his forties when he created the Ford Motor Company, and he had a number of failed companies under his belt. In fact, when Henry Ford Hospital was created, Ford had been part of the investment group that was building the Detroit General Hospital. In Ford's mind the project was a major failure—it was behind schedule and over budget. He became fed up with the endeavor, paid off the investors, and built the hospital on his own. That resilience is baked into what we do.

Between the Innovation Institute and thousands of individuals across Henry Ford, innovation has brought us eminence and the opportunity to make things better. In addition, our innovation efforts serve to reduce our costs, increase quality for patients, and even earn revenue to aid us in our not-for-profit mission of serving our community.

My job is to be an enabler of innovation, and I am proud of what we've accomplished. Almost anyone will tell you that "yes" is my favorite (and customary) response when someone comes to me with a new idea. I have engaged the board for funding on numerous occasions, and I don't mind sticking my neck out. And I take it as a good sign that I don't know everything that is going on here from an innovation standpoint. Sometimes I kid that I've lost all control of the organization because we are constantly developing so much that is new. One day in the cafeteria, for example, a woman came up to me to introduce a new employee. I said, "Well, where are you from?" She had moved here from Seattle to join our Global Health Initiative. I said to her, "I didn't know we had a Global Health Initiative."

Now I know that the program focuses on improving health care for underserved populations in places such as India, Peru, and Haiti. It has grown since that first conversation and I have learned much more about it. (For instance, we bring the best practices that we establish abroad back to Detroit to eliminate health-care disparity here.) But at the time, the initiative had acquired its own funding and proceeded without me knowing about it at all.

One of the key drivers that keeps innovation flowing for us is that we don't overanalyze and over manage it. Creative individuals need room to breathe. I put myself in that category, which is why I tend to identify with people who don't always follow the traditional path. I believe in trusting my instincts, attracting talented people, and giving them the structure and support—and sometimes the space—to do what they do best.

One of the things that I know about culture is that it can change on a dime. You have to manage it constantly. You cannot assume innovation will flourish simply because it has for decades. You have to always cultivate that culture. You have to continue to attract leaders who are going to carry on and provide the flexibility that allows employees to be entrepreneurial. Entrepreneurship can get swallowed up in a large organization. At a large health system like ours, it has to be part of our values. Learning and continuous improvement are also core values for us, and they reinforce innovation. When we are firing on all cylinders creativity emanates from everybody here—we are all trying to do a better job each day. I try very hard to enable that perfect condition. When it comes to innovation, my customary response has always been "*Yes.*"

CHAPTER FIVE

Make a Large Company Feel Small

One's own workers ought to be one's own best customers.

—Henry Ford

When I first arrived at Henry Ford, the head of human resources carried a small notebook. He brought it with him to meetings and kept it out on his desk. On the cover in black lettering it read: "Head Count." I was the only one who was appalled by this convention. Everyone else was accustomed to the notebook and phrase. It was common management parlance but it stuck in my craw like nothing else. I remember saying to him in a serious tone, "I don't ever want to hear that term again when we're talking about people." To me, the term *head count* refers to cattle or sheep. Maybe to chickens. But not ever to people. People are not interchangeable, and they are so much more than a number.

I thought that was the end of it—but it wasn't quite. I hired a new head of HR, who came over from Chrysler, and guess what? She started talking about head count. I said to her, "Kathy, we're talking about people here. That is not a phrase I have any interest in using in this organization." I never heard it again.

Now, obviously, I am a stickler about this. Yet, it is surprising to me that my perspective is unconventional—although I have found that it is. Organizations are forever focusing on many things at once—numbers, strategy, competition—and they forget that people are their foremost competitive advantage and responsibility. This is something that is ingrained in me and it has been the centerpiece of my leadership style from the beginning of my career. "People first" is my mantra, just as it was during the turnaround at Henry Ford and all through the Baldrige journey. HFHS is made up of twenty-three thousand individuals who are the caregivers, innovators, scientists, teachers, support staff, and leaders. Without them this organization would be devoid of character and, literally, empty.

Perhaps being in health care has colored my perspective more than if I were at the helm of a manufacturing company. After all, our service is caring for the sick. Without fundamental people skills, none of us in health care can be truly superb at what we do. That's where "people first" comes in—I believe that my job is to foster an organization that cares for the caregivers. It's one of the things that differentiates us from other health systems. Today, because of the work we've done, it's rare to find an employee at Henry Ford who isn't engaged in a positive way about creating a "people first" culture.

Henry Ford himself may have been more of a pragmatist than I am—I'm not entirely sure—but I do know that he stepped up and acted in ways that are relevant to creating a people-centered approach. First, of course, was offering the $5-per-day wage that helped establish the American middle class. That innovation stemmed the high turnover that so concerned Ford and expanded the market for Ford automobiles, even as it provided workers with a fair wage. Second, he paid considerable attention to the health and well-being of his employees when he built Henry Ford Hospital. He banned smoking by employees at the hospital, for example, which was a risky and unheard-of restriction at a time when smoking was ubiquitous.[1] He also built a beautiful solarium so people could benefit from the light and fresh air. And if you talk to the historians here, or to the Ford family, they will tell you that he created a culture where people felt like they were part of the family. Finally, Henry Ford Hospital was conceived with the common man in mind. Ford wanted to make sure that his autoworkers, the people who represented the working class, were able to access high-quality health care.

I am not asserting that Ford was a humanist, because there would be plenty of ways to refute that. What I *am* saying is that something about his worldview, which was unique in his time, is enormously appealing to me, namely, the idea that we need to take care of the workers in our community as well as those within our organization. If we do, they will be in a better position to pay it forward as they take care of others. Our vision at HFHS is to transform lives and communities through health and wellness—one person at a time. To me, that means putting systems into place to take care of the people in the organization. As Henry Ford knew, that is as good for organizational performance as it is for individual people.

Henry Ford's example was not the sole thing that fueled my passion for putting people first. When I was completing my administrative fellowship I remember running into Sam Tibbetts, the chair of the American Hospital Association. He asked me, "Nancy, why are you in this field?" I came up with a fast answer about why I was interested in health care personally and so on. His response to me was, "You know, Nancy, health care is all about people." We talked for a while and I have never forgotten that formative conversation. It has guided me. Healthcare professionals care for individuals in anxious, life-threatening situations and at the most desperate of moments. Their work affects people's lives. That fact impacts caregivers as well as patients. It is easy to come in to work at the hospital, get into a routine, and think of the job as normal. However, it is never really normal. When it comes to creating high-quality care across the health system, it's very clear to me that the way we take care of our employees connects directly to the way they take care of patients and their families. That idea is at the core of everything I do, and I am grateful that it came to me early on.

My philosophy, which informs my work at HFHS and at other systems and hospitals, bubbles up in five ways, which I will elaborate on here because they come together to provide an actionable framework for putting people first.

1. Treat doctors like housekeepers: with enormous dignity and respect
2. Care for the caregivers
3. Set people up to be their best
4. Inspire people
5. Make it personal

Treat Doctors Like Housekeepers: With Enormous Dignity and Respect

My parents were living in Lynchburg, Virginia, during my college years, so I spent one summer as a rotating intern at Lynchburg General Hospital. I worked in numerous departments doing frontline jobs, which helped to inform my understanding of—and empathy for—the challenging situations our staff are faced with every day. I was an ER clerk, a billing clerk, a human resources assistant, and so on. During my time there, when I was twenty years old, a prisoner walked up in shackles. I was the ER clerk and I remember registering the man. I was extremely nervous and trying to act normal, but my hands were shaking ever so slightly. These are the moments that stick with you. After that, when I finished college, I worked in a Florida hospital as a unit assistant, which was basically a combination of unit secretary and nurse aid. It was a minimum wage job that paid $3.50 an hour. I also worked as a switchboard operator on the weekends to make a little extra money. Both of these positions gave me more insight into the operations of a hospital than I could ever have realized at the time. I recall my time at Imperial Point Hospital in Fort Lauderdale vividly, not only because I learned so much so quickly, but also because it was the first time I saw a patient die in the ICU. I still remember his name.

Those experiences, as well as others, make me appreciate every person I have ever worked with in health care. But even more than appreciation, I developed a strong respect. That is what my "people first" focus is built on—respect. From what I've seen, there are very few people high up in the executive ranks of heath care who have been minimum wage workers in the industry. I think my earliest experiences in health care are at the core of the way I look at the world. When I was at the lowest rung, even with a college degree, I realized that every job is important and each one is difficult. The result is that I have respect for people, regardless of their title or job description. I tend to express that idea in this way: treat doctors like housekeepers—with incredible dignity and respect.

If you are consistent in your style of leadership, and are respectful of everyone; if you take the high road and constantly answer the "why" questions; if you treat people like adults, not children, and look them in the eye, you can avoid a lot of the bureaucracy and politics inherent in large organizations. This approach allows you to get to the heart of the matter—that organizations depend entirely on their people and vice versa.

What's more, respect is less about what you say and more about what you do. The most difficult times to put this into practice, for me, have been when performance is down and jobs are being eliminated. Looking people in the eye and talking them through the situation honestly is one way to show respect. If they are losing their job, explain why and tell them what is going to happen and when. Tell them about the supports that are in place for them and show some empathy. Another way to show respect is by fighting to protect as many jobs as you can. That can be very risky for any leader but it puts people above everything else. At Henry Ford, we made the difficult decision to close the Warren campus of our Henry Ford Macomb Hospital in early 2012, which could have meant layoffs for seven hundred people. That would have been the simplest way to handle the problem and was a logical plan. Instead, I was able to rally support to freeze job openings so that the displaced people could transition into open jobs across the system, as qualified.

I remember getting into a big debate with several of my colleagues. Our head of HR, who also happens to be a friend of mine, called me about the plan and said, "Nancy, I'm not sure we can do what you're asking us to do." I said, "Yes, we can. But we have to really want to do it. It's a lot more work but we can't lay these people off." In the end, the executive team agreed it was the right thing to do. We were in the midst of terrible regional unemployment. Many of our employees had spouses who were out of work. Putting more people on the street would have been devastating.

It took a tremendous amount of support from leaders across the system and considerable trust from the employees affected. In the end, however, every person who wanted to remain at HFHS was placed in a job. This kind of conviction and difficult decision making (Warren was one of three hospitals we closed over a fifteen-year period), combined with efforts to do the right thing for employees, shows how we put people first in the toughest of times.

Every business decision has a people component. Respecting each individual means minimizing the negative impact on those working within the organization. We are not in a production assembly line like Henry Ford's, making cars. We take care of people. Every job in health care is critically important. Sometimes a housekeeper comes into patients' rooms and interacts with them, and sometimes the front-desk clerk creates that first impression—in many ways these staff members are as critical as the physician performing the surgery. Every interaction counts and every person makes a difference.

Care for the Caregivers

When I talk about people, I'm referring to employees and physicians, as well as our patients and other customers—but I always start internally because it is so important that we care for the people who take care of others. The jobs that physicians and other employees do are not only high on the difficulty scale, as I've said, but they are also stressful, emotionally draining, and physically demanding. It's hard for caregivers to do this work in a positive way every single day when they're dealing with so much complexity of emotion.

With caregivers in mind, I knew as part of our No Harm Campaign we needed to look beyond patient care and strengthen the safety standards for the people working here. Employees in the health-care field are, after all, at risk for a wide range of hazards including back injuries caused by lifting patients, assorted sprains and strains, and dangerous infections, such as HIV and hepatitis, caused by accidental needle sticks. In addition, workplace violence is a major concern, as is depression induced by the high-stress environment. Many nurses and doctors go home at night worrying about their patients. They wonder, "Did I make a mistake? Did I make the right call?" It's important that we create an environment where people can do and feel their best. In this case, putting people first means creating systems to care for the health and well-being of caregivers.

As part of this effort, we focused first on encouraging self-reporting of injuries. We've long had access to worker's compensation information, but we didn't have much additional data. So, our head of human resources created a campaign that encouraged employees to report illness and injury. We added educational highlights in newsletters and e-news, developed an injury dashboard, and appointed a system safety officer to align safety functions to include employee harm. We also developed a workplace violence steering committee and a related internal crisis team to respond to emerging situations. As a result of our efforts to increase incident reporting for employee safety events, we achieved a 67 percent increase while decreasing actual harm events.

We also needed to find evidence-based ways to measure and respond to reporting by employees. Therefore, surveys and metrics guide our efforts to move the needle. For example, we mined the data and found that employee injuries from sharp instruments decreased by

14 percent in 2009. In addition, we saw a further 30 percent decrease in 2011.

Operational design is another critical tool for improving employee safety. In 2011, for example, we integrated five employee health clinics under one umbrella to increase efficiency, create consistency and standardization across the system, and promote access to care for employees. "Employee safety" became aligned with "employee health" efforts in 2011 to enable a more proactive and preventive approach with an intent to increase near-miss reporting while reducing injuries. Other efforts included developing mandatory education modules for employees and partnering with the public relations group to provide safety education.

A related way we care for our caregivers' well-being is by promoting work–life balance. Seventy-six percent of our employees are women, and many of them are mothers of young children. Others, including men, are often caring for a sick spouse, a disabled child, or an aging parent at home and then they come in during their shift to provide care for patients. Work–life balance is different for each person, of course, so we train managers and leaders to encourage employees to take care of themselves. As part of that, we teach "AIDET + 1" to all of our caregivers and have extended the training to apply to other employees. AIDET is a standard way of introducing oneself to a patient. The "+1" is about mindfulness of self and team. We teach staff to acknowledge that they have a lot going on in their lives and need to help and support one another. Part of the "+1" is focusing on building teamwork in units and departments and communicating with each other by first getting to know the "backstory" of the people on their team. Getting to know and understand each other helps us improve how we care for patients.

Finally, an important part of taking care of one's self is spending time with family or friends. I remind people to prioritize important occasions in their personal lives. Whether it's a special event at their child's school or even an important soccer game—they should be there. I badger them, as well, to take all of their vacation. Some leaders work long hours in order to make themselves seem indispensable—so much so that they don't take time off, let alone encourage others to do so. I've never fallen into that trap. I believe that it is important to be refreshed, spend time with family, and have a life outside of work. When people come back after taking time off, they're ten times stronger. I set a positive example by using all of my vacation and by encouraging physicians and employees to do the same.

Set People Up to Be Their Best

People want to succeed. My job as a leader is to create a culture where people can reach their full potential. In order to deliver on that, certain interconnected elements must be in place. Below, I offer a laundry list of things that I believe add up to this awesome ideal; in truth, the composition is more like that of a Rubik's Cube or mosaic than a list. There is no particular order here—these items feed into each other to carve space for people to be their best.

Say Yes

Many people at Henry Ford know that my favorite word is *yes*. I think of myself as both a cheerleader and a positive enabler, and I work to enable the disrupters as well as the everyday innovators. Whether we are talking about investing in leading-edge robotic operating rooms or using 3-D printing to design patient-perfect heart valves, I believe that individuals need room to build whatever they are most passionate about. And it is not just major innovations that need a runway for take-off. Many of the small wins we scored during our turnaround came from employees. That makes "yes" the most important word in my vocabulary.

Saying yes and relinquishing control requires a leap of faith. For example, a nurse in our dialysis center—an artist—came forward to her manager with an idea to paint her own colorful cartoons on the disposable hospital gowns worn by staff—that was an easy *yes—our leaders know that is what I would say!* People loved bringing art into the clinic and it cost us next to nothing. Now she does it every day and we use the gowns elsewhere in the system as well. The staff can't wait to see what she draws, and the gesture delights patients. It's reflexive to say no when an idea is off center, unusual, or expensive, but part of my job is reduce the risks of trying new things by being open to them. After all, people seldom come back twice with an idea. If a leader turns them away they aren't going to step up again. Supporting people's work (and dreams) is an important part of providing them with what they need to remain engaged and performing at their peak.

Be Apolitical

Many people consider political maneuvering to be an inherent part of organizational life. Forming coalitions, playing favorites, and doing backroom deals is a means for gaining support and getting things done. Some leaders even go so far as to encourage internal competition as a way to keep people on their toes. However, I work intentionally not to do that. I don't actively engage in or encourage politics. I don't wine and dine key board members in order to garner support for a proposal or plan. I take people to dinner to get to know them or to thank them for their effort, but I don't entertain unless it's authentic—something I want to do, not for personal gain.

More importantly, I don't play favorites. People can't be their best if they need to worry about "sucking up to the boss" or aligning themselves with the winning side. When I ask a question, I want an honest answer—not a political one. To me, avoiding politics means that I treat every person in the organization in the same way. One of our doctors said to me: "Nancy, I appreciate that you have equanimitas." That is exactly what I am trying to do and I believe that it sets the right tone for the rest of the organization.

Create a "Safe" Environment

I am not referring to hospital safety, but instead to an environment that is prepared for honesty, the free flow of ideas, and, more than anything else, a robust dialogue about mistakes that occur.

Years ago, when I was at Riverside Methodist in Columbus, Ohio, a chief nursing officer told me that he was firing the nurses who made mistakes. He wanted to run a tight ship, send the right signal, and so forth. I thought, "Oh great, you're creating a culture where no one will come forward and tell us when an error occurs." There is no perfect environment in health care, or anywhere else, just as there are no perfect people. When you're dealing with hundreds or thousands of individuals delivering care each day, all with their own human frailties and challenges, you need an environment where people feel comfortable reporting problems and mistakes. From what I've seen, there are, unfortunately, many hospitals that vastly underreport problems. The minute I see "no problems" reported, that is when I know there's a problem. It means people are not speaking up.

In addition to tracking and correcting the errors human beings inevitably make, you need to consider that the system or procedure may be the problem. People sometimes make mistakes, not because of their own ill intent but because a poor process creates space for mistakes. Without honesty and accurate reporting by individuals, there's no way to know when a process is broken.

Get Buy-In from Staff

Getting twenty-three thousand employees, physicians, and additional volunteers on the same page is critical. At the end of the day, my job comes down to guiding everyone's efforts in a common direction. To do that, goals need to be clearly communicated, and they need to resonate broadly. We've made some big bets on projects and investments in recent years: we built the expansive West Bloomfield health and wellness facility, invested over $300 million in the Henry Ford

Hospital campus, built an outpatient center in our downriver market, and invested $350 million in a new electronic medical health and records system. If people at Henry Ford did not feel connected to these priorities, it would have been impossible to see these special projects through while running day-to-day operations.

In almost every case, we made these projects system-wide priorities that everyone could support. For instance, as we built the West Bloomfield center we set up a warehouse complete with mock operating rooms, emergency rooms, and patient rooms. We encouraged patients, family members of patients, physicians, nurses, and support staff to come in and critique them—and thousands did. They told us what they liked and disliked, and how we could do better. When you get people involved and invested they think: "Okay, I'm a part of this." In our case, it wasn't just the West Bloomfield team that felt a strong sense of ownership—the entire system owned that project. The same was true during our recent IT installation. We rolled it out all across the system and had leaders from each hospital helping the others. When you're setting big priorities, it's vital to give people ways to engage even beyond their own business units.

I've been in work environments where each group owned their own projects and everyone else heard about it secondhand. As a result, people resented investments made in other parts of the organization. I've learned to be clear about the priorities and why they are important. Part of making this work involves answering the why questions: Why are we putting the money into this? Why does it strengthen our position in the marketplace? Why is this helping us?

If people understand the larger context, it's easier for them to buy in. With that idea in mind, we include our communication team in the planning and execution of every new strategy. We use multiple channels in the rollout because we know that not everyone reads the employee newsletter or looks at the e-mail exchanges or participates in social media. I get personally involved and we mix it up in terms of our communication channels: I do videos, blog posts, and town hall meetings. I've got an interview technique for our vodcast, where I bring leaders in, and we sit down and talk about an initiative. People see the ideas exchanged in a more interactive and interesting format.

Take Training and Development Seriously

The last über agenda item for setting people up to be their best is creating training opportunities. Typically, training is the first place most organizations cut when they are strapped for cash. But we've always maintained funding for training programs, regardless of any ebb and flow in our overall financial performance. This is a fundamental way that we demonstrate a commitment to our people. We've never pulled back on employee development, leadership development, professional training, or availability of courses in Henry Ford Health System University. This includes making mentoring a priority for everyone. I have had a number of amazing mentors who helped me throughout my career, and I am always mentoring multiple people in the organization. I expect the same from every other leader.

As a result, there are so many examples of people who started their careers in housekeeping or dietary but who are now nurses or leaders in the organization. Training and development fosters loyalty and keeps people engaged and growing.

Setting People Up to Succeed

Setting people up to succeed is a big job. I have touched on some of my priorities above, but following is a longer list, from the Gallup Q12 survey that we use at HFHS, comprised of success factors that I believe can make a real difference.

An employee . . .

- Knows what is expected of them at work
- Has the materials and equipment needed to do their work right

- Has the opportunity to do what they do best every day
- Receives recognition or praise for doing good work at least once a week
- Perceives that their supervisor, or someone at work, cares about them as a person
- Perceives that someone at work encourages their development
- Perceives that their opinions seem to count at work
- Understands how the mission or purpose of the company makes them feel their job is important
- Observes their associates or fellow employees being committed to doing quality work
- Has someone talk to them about their progress at least twice a year
- Has had an opportunity within the past year at work to learn and grow

Inspire People

People need to feel inspired in order to be at their best in a pressure-cooker environment like the one we experience in health care, or myriad other high-stress industries. The three ways that I think about inspiring and being inspired are through leadership, philanthropy, and aesthetics.

As a leader, I know that my actions have a direct and immediate impact on people across the organization. There is a ripple effect that occurs based on my words and actions. Every leader knows that "bad leadership" is the number-one reason people leave their jobs to work elsewhere. Such moves have little to do with financial compensation—people want to be inspired.

There are a lot of ways that I try to inspire confidence and high performance, but one thing that I feel is especially important is to take every person seriously. This is something that became apparent to me when I was twelve. I was in eighth grade when I started writing to colleges. My sister was getting ready to go away to school so I took the opportunity to think about my own future and express my interest. I wrote to a number of schools but the only one that responded was Duke University. And guess where I went to school when the time arrived? Yes, Duke University. Why? Because they took me seriously.

Giving proper weight to people's ideas and concerns is just one of the many ways that I as a leader try to inspire people to be their best. Offering opportunities for philanthropy and volunteerism is another way. This is particularly true in an organization such as Henry Ford, where our strong connection to the city of Detroit defines us and sets us apart. Philanthropy, then, is one of our core activities and it is part of what sustains our business. As part of our mission to give back to the city, we have a number of campaigns through which employees donate their time and money. Leaders across the company are expected to step up—and they do so wholeheartedly in order to set the right example for everyone else.

The numerous ways in which we give back to the community are a key part of what draws people to work here. And many of our charitable and philanthropic programs are noteworthy: we have school-based health clinics across Detroit, for example, together with mobile vans that deliver preventive care and medical treatments to kids and families. Employees and physicians take a lot of pride in these programs, as well as in the many other ways we engage the community. We have a Community Giving Campaign that routinely raises over $3 million each year for HFHS, United Way, and Black United Fund, with 60 percent participation by employees and physicians—number one in the country. We also endorse special campaigns that encourage all employees to generously support charitable causes in the community to the best of their ability, from the American Heart Association Heart Walk to walks for the American Diabetes Association and the National Kidney Foundation. I view these philanthropic initiatives as ways to build community partnerships *and* employee engagement. As a result, we have thousands of HFHS walkers at our events. One example that stands out is our commitment to the local Heart Walk; over 11 years, we raised nearly $4 million, and were recognized almost annually for raising more than any other health system in the country and often more than any company. This kind of achievement happens because people really believe in what we are doing, it aligns with their values, and they find a sense of joy and purpose in helping others. That's inspiring.

The final way I believe it is possible to inspire people is through the healing arts. When I started as CEO at Henry Ford Hospital, our chair of surgery, Dr. Scott Dulchavsky, took me on a tour of Detroit Receiving Hospital. I recall that it had one of the most spectacular art collections I had ever seen. I remembered art displayed prominently at other institutions I had worked at as well, from Memorial Sloan Kettering in New York to Duke University Hospital, but Henry Ford Health System had next to nothing at the time. I saw that as an opportunity to do better. Together, Scott and I began working on a process to bring a few signature pieces to Henry Ford Hospital. We met with local artists. We started a board philanthropic fund to support the healing arts. We worked with the Detroit Institute of Art to secure art on loan. We've even worked with the Detroit Symphony to bring music into Henry Ford.

This is something that's near and dear to me because I am personally inspired by the arts. Based on the feedback I've received from employees and patients, I'm not alone. The art we have on display now across the health system and the music we've brought in for our staff, patients, and guests is just beautiful, and their mere presence creates a better atmosphere. It has really transformed the environment for delivering and receiving health care.

Make It Personal

When my mother met someone, she would forever remember the person's name. She had perfect recall about what people told her concerning their family and personal interests. She would ask questions and

CHAPTER SEVEN

Detroit: Partner for Renewal

...In conclusion, I will state that it is my intention...to go forward with plans for a complete and credible hospital for the benefit of Detroit.

—Henry Ford, from his letter to the
board of the Detroit General
Hospital Association, June 1, 1914

When I joined Henry Ford in 1998, almost everyone else was rushing in the opposite direction. People were leaving Detroit in droves, and some seemed shocked that I was excited about joining Henry Ford. They would ask, "Why did you come here?" I always replied, "I'm here because I'm working for a great leader, Gail Warden at Henry Ford. I am here because Henry Ford is a national model for health care. And I'm here because I really like Detroit." The common refrain was: "Really? You like Detroit?"

through the years, we always make this a major event. If needed, I would pay for the night myself—that's how much it means to employees and their families.

The other recognition program I'll mention is one that I created at Akron City Hospital called SuggestQuest, which challenged people to step up with ideas to make things better. Over the years, we delivered some big financial awards to clinical teams and individuals who proposed improvements that either saved money for the hospital or enhanced the patient experience. And we made a big deal out of these awards—with the whole team, myself included, gathering around to present the prize. This might seem insignificant in an environment where lives are on the line, but I can tell you that it makes an impression on people when the COO walks up with balloons in her hand to make a personal presentation. It is well-deserved recognition delivered with a personal touch. It not only rewards innovation but it also encourages people to perform better when the pressure is on.

Part of the success of "making it personal" is a willingness to really listen to staff. That may mean reversing a decision that negatively impacts them, something that a lot of leaders refuse to do. Fairly recently, we announced the closing of our child-care center. It was losing $300,000 a year and we only had twenty-two employees with children enrolled. It turned out that the employees who used it really needed it in order to work their shift. The issue went viral and there was a mini uprising. We addressed the situation as a team and we were able to turn it into something positive. Now, the employees who are most affected are helping us with marketing strategies and we're working together to recruit new families and keep the center open without health system funding. What I heard after we backed off on closing the center was that people felt heard. Child care is a major issue for parents. It's personal. Reversing a decision and thinking through new options requires effort and sacrifice; in cases like this it goes a long way toward creating an environment where people feel that their personal needs are being met.

Putting people first, in all the ways I have mentioned, is not just my passion. It is my job. As a chief executive I am the individual responsible for connecting the dots. Focusing on people, then, ultimately equates to improving performance. Taking a genuine interest in your people pays incredible dividends for the organization—in fact, it's the best performance strategy you could possibly have. When staff are engaged, they will engage with customers directly and in a positive way. When they are engaged, they will help you improve your organization. They will produce new ideas, they will create greater efficiencies, and they will drive financial success.

I put people first and I would like to believe that I attract other leaders who do the same. This is the legacy I want for myself at Henry Ford and everywhere that I have been fortunate enough to make my mark.

CHAPTER SIX

Being Different: The Strength of Diversity

I grew up in the '60s and '70s, when it seemed as if the nation was on fire with change and conflict. Like so many others at the time, I became fixated on the civil rights movement, the race riots around the country, and the aftermath of the assassinations of John F. Kennedy, Martin Luther King Jr., and Bobby Kennedy. I recall that feeling of sadness and utter disbelief when King was shot. It was jarring. Yet, I always felt comforted to have parents like mine, who were open-minded and progressive in their thinking about race. I always felt they stood on the right side of the divide. My mother, in particular, as both a teacher and an individual, was aligned with King's message on judging people by the content of their character, rather than the color of their skin, and his perspective on combating racial inequality through nonviolence.

More than anything, they both set a positive example for me and my sisters and brother, and they wanted us to understand the implications of what was going on around us. In fact, civil rights and the related issues were common topics at the dinner table when we finished discussing our day at school. I loved to spread the newspaper out on the floor—it was so big that I couldn't hold it but I pored over as much of it as I could. Because it was such a caustic and vibrant time, I have certain personal memories that have stuck with me, and that show how the era is imprinted on my mind.

The first memory is of a lovely woman, Isa May, who cleaned our house once a week and helped care for us kids when my mother was in the hospital. One day, during the race riots, Isa May couldn't get a bus to her house and we went with my dad to drop her off. I remember looking around at the neighborhood where she lived and feeling the anger rising from people. It was eye-opening to realize how some people in my hometown lived and the emotions they felt, and at the same time I recall feeling concerned about Isa May's safety.

The second flash encompasses memories of some of the kids I grew up with in my town, and how I came to see that their world was different from mine. In elementary school I had a very good friend who was Filipina: Marie Lim. I used to go to Marie's house to play and she came over to mine. There were very few Asian kids in the public schools at that time and there was lingering anti-Asian sentiment left over from World War II. It took me a while to see that sentiment—but when I did I realized that it was palpable. I had another friend whose parents were deaf. The eldest child in her family, my friend had an incredible maturity and was always doing things that seemed beyond her age. She assumed responsibilities and took care of her family in ways that I never had to. Finally, I remember Marvin Weinberger, a Jewish boy who played the violin with me as part of a quartet. Even in Akron, Ohio, I saw firsthand that Jews weren't yet accepted in many places in the way that I was.

The third major recollection that I have centers on an incident that occurred while I was in college, when my youngest sister, Joan, was a teenager and my parents were living in Lynchburg, Virginia. Joan became friends with an African American girl from our church, and we were all acquainted with the family. We knew the father of the family particularly well, because he worked two jobs, including waiting tables at a club where my parents belonged. One day my mother saw him at the club and gave him a hug. Things changed for us in that instant. The room fell silent. By the looks she received you would have thought she had committed a crime. After that, people looked upon my parents with a degree of suspicion. This was the South in the '70s, and white people didn't go around hugging African American waiters. After that, my parents couldn't get out of Virginia fast enough. A few years later they moved back to Ohio, but that experience in Virginia was one that none of us could forget.

These are some of the episodes that forged my thinking about difference and diversity. The truth is that I lived a fairly sheltered life as a young child, but my own advantages only served to underscore for me that not everyone around me enjoyed the same equality. My parents judged people based on the content of their character, and their words and deeds, rather than the color of their skin. But that, again, is part of what helped me see that the world did not always work that way.

What I Know About Diversity

I am always so proud when I recall my mother's socially progressive perspective on race and gender roles. She was way ahead of her time. But the vision I had of her wavered for a moment, a little later in life, and it threw me for a loop. My mother was extremely sick at the time and she was undergoing dialysis at Akron City Hospital where I had previously worked. I was there with her, offering support, along with my dad. We wanted to get as much time with her as we could. It was a difficult year for me, even beyond my mother's illness. I had been outed, through the anonymous letter sent to my boss and the hospital board members at Riverside Methodist Hospital—and the experience was still fresh on my mind. Then, out of the blue, with other people standing nearby including former colleagues that I knew, my mom looked at me, and said in a loud voice: "Nothing would appall me more than if you were a lesbian." I couldn't believe it. I felt shattered and traumatized—it was overwhelming for me.

Later, on that same day, when I was back in her room, she said something that offered a clue about where she was coming from. She said, "Nancy, I am so afraid for you." And I could tell that she meant it. She had spent her whole life telling me that I could be anything I wanted—I could do whatever I set my mind to. She was so proud of my career and I think she lived vicariously through me in that sense. It was the type of career she always wanted for herself, unencumbered by gender barriers and stereotypes. And then, to know that I was gay— she was terrified that it might cost me my career and that I would lose everything.

I said, "Mom, I'm going to be okay." I think that made her feel a little better. But the reality was that *I* was not sure it would be okay for me right then. It was one of the times when I wondered if I would be able to achieve my potential and do the things I wanted to do. Having kept the truth secret for twenty years, I felt like I was living two lives. This was a time of reckoning.

Personally, I was feeling isolated. Almost no one knew for certain that I was gay because I hadn't come out to my family. They strongly suspected, of course, because I had lived with my first partner for fifteen years. And even long before that, as a kid, I loved wearing boys' clothing, and I forever wanted to play with my brother's toys. My mother always went along with it, no questions asked. She even bought me the men's watch I picked out when it was time for me to have a nice dress watch. But we never talked about it. Professionally, I felt like I couldn't entirely be myself either. I believed for a time that the only way that I could confidently pursue my dreams was to compartmentalize my life and work. I looked around at the people in my profession, and "hospital administration" didn't exactly seem like a gay enclave. In fact, business in general was not a place where you found many openly gay people. It was a lonely existence from this perspective, and the secrecy had put a lot of stress on my relationship with my partner. In addition, having my career derailed—even for a moment—was jarring. I never thought I would get married and have a typical life with a partner, and that put a very heavy burden on me to succeed in my career and provide for myself.

But it all came together for me personally and professionally. There were many moments when I could see that my mother fully accepted me. She gave my partner presents, for instance, and she was genuinely happy when we were together around her. Then, right before she passed away, she made a toast to me. We were at a lovely resort in West Virginia, the Greenbrier. This was about ten days before she died, and we knew she wasn't going to live much longer. She raised her glass and she said, "Nancy, they don't deserve you." I will never forget that as long as I live. I could tell that she really understood what I was going through and it lightened my load immensely.

My dad, who never really said much at all about my sexuality then, is open about his acceptance of me today. At his age (93), it's pretty remarkable. He tells me all the time how happy he is that I married Pam and that we have a family.

Although that was a difficult time in my life, it was a positive turning point for me. After my experience at Riverside Methodist and my struggle to be honest with my family and friends, I realized that I was ready to be more open. Hiding my true self was counter to everything I believed. If the times had been different, perhaps I would have acted sooner, I'm not sure. Regardless, I was ready to be out in the open. That is what I have done ever since and I have never looked back—and I've most certainly never regretted my decision. Somewhat surprisingly, I have enjoyed enormous support from my mentors, colleagues at HFHS, and family. In turn, I have been able to step up and support many other people by fostering a culture—particularly at Henry Ford—that values people for who they are and helps them leverage their unique gifts to be their best.

Leaning In

As much as I struggled with being open about my sexuality, I had very little doubt and trepidation about putting myself out there as a female leader surrounded by male counterparts. Although I agree that being a woman makes it more difficult to reach the highest peaks in an organization, I managed to not let that hold me back. In some cases, in fact, I have had access to significant opportunities *because* I was a woman. Having a big job at a young age offered advantages. When I was COO at Akron City Hospital, for example, I was invited to be a member of the board at the First National Bank of Ohio. I was one of two women on the board. More notably, I was thirty-two years old, while everyone else was well past fifty.

In terms of public boards, I've often been the first or the second woman to serve. Unfortunately, though, we still have a very long way to go in bringing women into the highest levels of leadership. What's interesting is that if you look at board recruitment today, people are out there searching for women to improve their record on diversity. At Walgreens we have three women on the board now, and it's a game changer. When you're the only woman, or even one of two, you're always in that mode of needing to put your best foot forward. You are proving yourself. When you have three women on the board, your voices are collectively forceful enough to bring a different perspective. You can take more risks. And it's much better for customers when a board more accurately represents the consumer dynamic.

Personally, I grew accustomed to being surrounded by men. I wanted to help change that, of course, and I've done a lot over the years with that goal in mind. But when I was in my thirties and forties I just thought, "I've got to prove myself. I've got to be better than the rest to make sure I don't lose this spot."

That said, I am quick to admit that I had an advantage for most of my career that many women can't claim: I wasn't married with kids. I didn't think having children was an option for me, so that eliminated the trade-off aspect many women face and simplified the work–life conundrum that I would otherwise have had to manage. In my career, and in most careers in health care, you have to be willing to move because the next job opportunity is not always going to be in your backyard. But it's tough to move a family. It's tough to pull kids out of school. I always had geographical flexibility, which allowed me to develop my career more easily.

With that advantage, I have always leaned in, and I believe that there is some truth to the overall lean-in philosophy. By that I mean I believe women overall would benefit, and advance further in organizations, if more of us courageously pursued our career coals. A few years back, in fact, I noticed that some women were not expecting as much from their careers as men; therefore, they were not pushing as hard for opportunities. I also saw that some women had very narrow criteria for what they would do next, so they were not as available for opportunities. Finally, women at one time tended to avoid negotiating for themselves. Instead, they were looking out for others, carrying the heavier burden on family issues, and tended to be too easily satisfied on the pay side. More recently, I've gotten a very different sense of young women. They are learning from the women who came before them, they are asking for opportunities, and they are more aggressive in pay negotiations. As a result, we'll hopefully see some of the pay disparities narrow over time. And as the pipeline of women leaders increases, these new executives and political leaders will create a path for others. In addition, they will continue to change the structure and norms of organizations.

This is not to say that my career advancement has been a breeze. In fact, the first fifteen years were the trickiest in terms of routing around gender biases. It wasn't exactly an open door for women getting into hospital administration. And it was a double whammy for me—a gay woman. When I was in college, for example, and even after that, there were numerous individuals in the field who were not particularly supportive of a woman advancing into leadership. They tried to dissuade me and at times belittle me. The good news is that it spurred me on. Somebody telling me I can't do something is always the best motivator. In addition, once I got my graduate degree and was working on my residency and fellowship, I found mentors who were interested in me and supportive of my aspiration to lead a large organization. They went out on a limb for me, and their support is one of the reasons I work so hard.

Why Diversity Works

I have always tried to foster a workforce that demonstrates a strong commitment to diversity. The personal experiences I elaborated upon above are an obvious part of the reason I believe that diversity, in all its forms, is vital to organizational success. However, there are other reasons as well.

First, it has become clear to me that a diverse workforce allows people to maximize their unique potential, which makes organizations more competitive. For example, diversity enables people with disparate talents to showcase them—in a large, complex organization, complementary talents are always more desirable than overlapping ones. The converse is also true: a homogenous culture delivers people with similar capabilities, thereby leaving organizations deep in the same few skills and experiences and very exposed elsewhere.

Like many CEOs, I have seen firsthand that diverse teams are a catalyst for innovation. Solving seemingly intractable problems, after all, requires bringing different types of people together. To me, diversity goes beyond race, gender, ethnicity, and sexual orientation. Hiring individuals with nontraditional backgrounds, for instance, brings into the organization the type of intellectual diversity that channels breakthrough thinking. Gerard van Grinsven is an excellent example of this thinking; he had no health-care experience whatsoever, so he was not the most likely candidate to lead our new Henry Ford West Bloomfield Hospital when I hired him. Yet, his status as an "outsider" was a main reason the hospital achieved its ambitious goals of becoming a premier health and wellness facility. We had plenty of health-care experts on staff at the time. It was Gerard's unique expertise in creating luxury-inspired experiences for Ritz-Carlton that made all the difference in allowing innovation to flourish. In other words, Gerard and other unorthodox hires at Henry Ford have worked in our favor specifically because they disrupted the norm—not despite the fact that they did so.

We have seen the same dynamic when our health plan and medical groups collaborate to solve problems. The people at the health plan have a completely different perspective than clinicians do, and vice versa. When you get them together, both groups maximize learning: physicians are exposed to the rapidly changing dynamics of payment and benefits management, and individuals from the health plan come to understand the vast challenges of providing quality care for patients. Putting all the pieces together has yielded innovations for us related to health education and wellness, improved technology for prescribing medicine, and even better disease management.

The last, and arguably most important, reason to value diversity (particularly in an environment like that of Henry Ford Health System) is to meet the needs of the community. Detroit's population of roughly 713,000 people is 83 percent African American and 8.6 percent Hispanic or Latino. In addition, Arab Americans of Lebanese, Palestinian, and Syrian ethnicities call Detroit home.[1] And this heritage goes way back: by 1916, in fact, Henry Ford had more than 550 Syrian employees, including many recent Muslim immigrants, working in his factories in Detroit.[2] If our organization did not reflect that longstanding diversity, we would not be in a position to earn the trust of our multicultural patients. For example, most Muslim women require female doctors, and all-female attendants, at childbirth. It's very intentional, then, that we have female physicians, advanced practice nurses, and midwives who are engaged in clinics to serve the Arab American community.

The long and short of it is that diversity in health care is enormously relevant because it affects the ways we deliver care. And our community is getting ever more diverse, so from a strictly business perspective, some of our greatest growth potential lies in serving diverse communities. We want to make sure that we are known as a place that is extremely open, welcoming, and receptive to the special interests and needs of those communities. There's a cause and effect here that becomes apparent when you connect the dots.

How to Do Diversity

In order to create an organization where diversity is a central tenet, inclusion needs to be considered in all major decisions. And the culture needs to be such that all employees have an opportunity for advancement, are treated with respect and dignity, and can contribute their diversity of thought, work style, background, and experiences. That is a lot to accomplish, and it requires effort in short bursts as well as ongoing determination. The rest of this chapter outlines that ways that I, along with others at HFHS, approach making a diverse organization that serves the needs of twenty-three thousand staff as well as the larger community.

Define Diversity Broadly

In the context of organizational diversity, it is mission critical to take into account the many dimensions that extend beyond race, ethnicity, sexual orientation, and gender. Diversity encompasses not only these important differences but also more subtle dimensions such as work style, lifestyle, physical capacity, behavioral differences, and other human characteristics. And even beyond human workforce characteristics, diversity is highly relevant as it pertains to the workplace, the marketplace, and even the organizational structure. In keeping with our progressive approach at Henry Ford, we define diversity broadly and apply the following principles that serve to extend the way we think about it:

- Sensitivity to family structure and lifestyles
- The health and well-being of employees
- Flexibility for accomplishing work assignments
- An organizational culture that supports and leverages the talent and skills of all employees
- Recognition and respect for efforts and contributions of all employees
- Social responsibility and commitment to community

One of my personal favorites to foster is cognitive diversity—or thinking differently. As I mentioned earlier, my mentor Al Gilbert had a notable capacity to work effectively with physicians. Although this is a bit more radical, he also valued the perspective of individuals who were branded as "troublemakers." If an employee gained a reputation for going against the grain, Al would really listen. Al knew that these people were thinking differently, and that they might have something valuable to impart. This is an unconventional practice that I have emulated. Disrupters are not necessarily beloved by their managers or HR, but they have different perspectives that are worth hearing. Diverse thinking is hard to come by, and it is often an undervalued or misunderstood type of diversity that can make any organization better.

Maintaining a broad definition of diversity not only creates a bigger safety net for individuals in your organization, it also helps leaders remove the barriers to difference so that it can be valued and leveraged.

Look for People Who Are Underutilized

When I was at Riverside Methodist Hospital I got to know an African American gentleman named Zakaria Nyongesa who was an assistant parking supervisor for us on the weekends. He was an insightful, humble, and fascinating individual who did a fine job. But I had a hunch that his talents were being wasted, so I struck up a conversation with him. It went like this:

"Zak, tell me about yourself," I said.

"Nancy, you know, I have a PhD," he replied.

"You do?" I said, "What is it in?"

"It's in African studies. I teach at Ohio State part-time."

"That's amazing. What are you doing as a parking supervisor?"

"Well, I just needed a second job."

"Really?"

After that, I couldn't stop thinking about Zak. When I was working on the front lines at hospitals in roles such as admitting clerk and nurse's aide, I saw so many talented people like Zak who were being underutilized. These were people who didn't have a big title or status but who had training, ideas, and experience that would have helped us if we could have put them to work in the right roles. Sometimes they needed encouragement to further their training or finish their degree, but many other times they simply needed to be given a chance.

I spent a lot of time with Zak and created a job for him as our first director of diversity. This was more than twenty years ago, when Riverside was informally known as "The Riverside Hilton." It was not especially racially diverse or progressive in terms of diversity practices; therefore, appointing Zak was a major move. I recall African American nurses and others saying to me, "Nancy, do you really want to do this?" The appointment was counter to the culture they were accustomed to working in. The amazing thing was that Zak, and the people he brought in to help him, changed the organization for the better. Together, we created the type of change that was long past due.

Another person I met around that time at Riverside was Wanda Dillard. Wanda was trained in respiratory therapy, served in the military, and was an evening shift manager in the process of earning an advanced degree. An African American woman, Wanda confided in me that people often said very subtle things to her that were intended to cut her down. When I got to know her I found that she had an incredible passion for community development. I become a mentor to Wanda and in time I made her director of community health. Again, it was a game changer at Riverside. Later, Ohio State hired Wanda to set up a community development program similar to the one she had created for me at Riverside.

Part of diversity, for me, is creating new ways to take better advantage of people's gifts and talents. The best way that I know to do this is to look for individuals in the organization who are underutilized and open doors for them. I acknowledge that this can be a high-risk, high-reward approach. It doesn't pan out every time, but when it does it can make an important difference in the organization and send a powerful message that talent and diversity really matter.

Create Support Structures

While opening doors for people who are different is important, diversity also requires an active commitment to creating formal and informal support structures. Many diverse candidates have either been discouraged, like Wanda, or denied advancement, just as I was when I was forced to walk away from my job after being outed as a lesbian. When that type of thing happens, many people feel discouraged and isolated. As a gay person, for instance, I grew accustomed to hearing comments and jokes about gay people. Before I was strong enough to speak up, I remained silent. At times, these episodes made me feel powerless and alone. Although I never let the attitudes I encountered hold me back, the reality is that I could have been tremendously impacted by these negative forces. Fortunately, I have received support, from my family, who encouraged me when I was growing up, to numerous mentors all through my training and career who have opened doors and guided me to the next opportunity. They saw something in me and they opened their hearts and their minds to what I could do.

Because of the chances I have had and because I understand the power of support structures, I always give back, supporting others the way that I was supported. Regardless of my personal passion for encouraging difference, and my desire to be an active mentor, making diversity work at HFHS was a system-wide priority that started before I arrived and will be ongoing when my successor, Wright Lassiter III, takes over as chief executive.

At Henry Ford, informal support for diversity includes mentorship, sponsorship, and full inclusion, and this practice opens doors for diverse employees. More formal support includes training programs, networking opportunities, and employee resource groups (ERGs) for those who are Hispanic/Latino, of Middle Eastern descent, African American, or LGBT, as well as for members of other diverse and minority groups. Employee resource groups at Henry Ford provide professional and personal growth opportunities and peer networking, as well as education and awareness for participants and other employees around various dimensions of diversity.

Diversity will always be the foundation on which Henry Ford Health System stands, and in many ways diversity defines us. The culture and the support structures contribute to making it possible for people to work here in an open, safe, and honest manner. Unencumbered by fear, they can bring their best selves to work.

Consider All Stakeholders

Just as it's important to apply a broad definition to diversity itself, so, too, should we apply the ideals of diversity beyond the workforce to include all the stakeholders in health care, including patients and their families as well as neighbors, community partners, and suppliers. Let's look at how HFHS applies this principle, because we have dedicated considerable time and resources to develop best practices in the area of diversity.

In terms of striving for culturally appropriate and inclusive care for patients and their families, we look for insight from the Institute on Multicultural Health at Henry Ford, led by Dr. Kimberlydawn Wisdom and Dr. Denise White-Perkins. Both are nationally known physicians and health disparity experts who have shaped the vision for the institute, which seeks to improve the health and quality of life for underrepresented racial and ethnic populations and to eliminate health care–related disparities. The institute approaches this goal by conducting research to identify health disparities and gaps in care for minority groups, and it disseminates outcomes locally, regionally, and nationally, developing community-based programs aimed at improving the health of underrepresented populations. It also offers training to improve the cultural competence of researchers and health-care providers. For instance, it works with hearing-impaired patients and their families to determine how to improve the quality of care with respect to the patients' preferences and special needs. In addition, it looks at how the socioeconomic status of minority groups impacts health and health care.

HFHS's diversity programs don't stop with the needs of patients and their families, however. We have a diversity initiative designed to provide all suppliers, including women entrepreneurs and minority-owned businesses, with equal access to procurement and contracting opportunities within the organization. An inclusive and transparent sourcing process ensures that we seek the most talented, innovative, experienced, and cost-competitive suppliers available. Doing business with diverse suppliers makes good business sense and it contributes to the financial stability of the many local communities to which Henry Ford delivers health-care services.

I'm proud that Henry Ford is recognized locally and nationally for both its multicultural care and its supplier diversity initiative—and both are best practices in the health-care industry.

Require Diversity at the Top

Leadership is still the most challenging arena for diversity, and yet it is arguably the most important when it comes to altering the way society and organizations think about equality. Diversity at the top of an organization is a challenge for a number of reasons: the pipeline of diverse candidates is not as robust as it should to be, leaders continue to mentor and promote people with backgrounds that are similar to their own, and, in many cases, diversity at the executive level is not mandated.

At HFHS, we tend to rely on internal staff for many of our leadership-level searches because the top executive search firms in Chicago and New York don't send us enough minority candidates to satisfy our diversity requirements. This has been the case for as long as I can remember. Our community is highly diverse, while our leadership is not as diverse as our community. With that in mind, we challenged ourselves to catalyze diversity at the top. For example, we've mandated that at least 20 percent of employees in Henry Ford leadership training academies and succession plans must be women and minorities. In addition, candidates interviewed for director- and board-level positions must reflect the diversity of the available applicant pool and the communities that we serve. We also provide mandatory cultural-competency training to our entire workforce, including physicians and leaders.

Is this enough? Probably not, but it's a solid start and we've witnessed some positive results. When I arrived in Detroit, for instance, only two of Henry Ford's senior leaders were women. Today, there are sixteen—that is a huge step forward and I am incredibly proud of our progress. To be frank, however, I think the dramatic increase in female leaders here has less to do with our concerted effort to recruit women and more to do with the fact that they are looking at our organization and saying, "This is an enlightened place. This is where I want to be."

Despite notable progress, I would say that we have achieved more modest improvement in hiring African Americans for top leadership roles. But that may change quickly when my successor, Wright Lassiter III, who is African American, takes the helm in 2016. As our new CEO, I suspect that he will enhance our ability to attract top talent from the African American community, just as my presence likely helped attract more of the best women. Wright is an exceptional fit to lead Henry Ford. His experience running a diverse health system, his considerable leadership talents, and his alignment with our core values are just three of the reasons my board and I chose Wright as my successor.

Be Intentional

In order to continue to make progress, we need to mindfully cultivate the diversity pipeline and make sure we are bringing in people—whether they are filling administrative or clinical roles—who are capable of providing top leadership for systems and hospitals. And I believe that we can do it. Henry Ford has been the easiest place I've ever worked to build a diverse team of leaders because we're so mission focused and community minded. That is what earned us the number-one spot on DiversityInc's 2015 list of most diverse health systems in the country.

Is the fact that a gay woman is leading the organization another reason we are seeing some progress in recruiting diverse candidates to fill top roles? Perhaps. Reaching a tipping point is an uphill battle, but once you are there it becomes simpler to maintain. In order for our industry to get over that hump, and become better, we need to continue to make diversity in top leadership roles a priority. A hospital or a health system is very much like a city or a community: by its nature, it is incredibly complicated and diverse. We need to be attentive to those aspects of our environment or we can't serve patients, employees, or other stakeholders nearly as well as we would like and they deserve.

The common denominator in leadership diversity, and indeed in all types of diversity, is an intentional commitment. For us, diversity is built into every pillar of performance that we focus on at Henry Ford. What that serves to do is embed diversity into our strategies. For example, a component of our focus on quality is eliminating racial disparities in health care. Every initiative has a diversity element, whether it's supplier diversity or an employee resource group that supports the gay community—it all creates more ways for people to feel supported, valued, and able to reach their full potential.

CHAPTER SEVEN

Detroit—Partner for Renewal

...In conclusion, I will state that it is my intention...to go forward with plans for a complete and credible hospital for the benefit of Detroit.

> —Henry Ford, from his letter to the
> board of the Detroit General
> Hospital Association, June 1, 1914

When I joined Henry Ford in 1998, almost everyone else was rushing
in the opposite direction. People were leaving Detroit in droves, and
some seemed shocked that I was excited about joining Henry Ford.
They would ask, "Why did you come here?" I always replied, "I'm
here because I'm working for a great leader, Gail Warden at Henry
Ford. I am here because Henry Ford is a national model for health care.
And I'm here because I really like Detroit." The common refrain was:
"Really? You like Detroit?"

Detroit—A Love Story

Yes, I really do like Detroit. Detroit has always felt like home to me. When I was young, my family visited the city and the memory stayed with me. Coming from Akron, Detroit seemed like a big metropolis with so much to offer. Yet, that impression aside, Akron and Detroit have some striking similarities. Both have been one-industry towns, by and large—Akron had the rubber industry and Detroit the automotive. Historically, they've both had not only a strong middle class but also enduring opportunities that allowed working class individuals to support their families and have a great life. Both have a major union presence, too. Finally, corporations have invested significantly in these communities, allowing them to develop culturally in ways that they would not have otherwise.

The vibe in Detroit, as well, suits me in a number of ways. I've always considered myself to be pretty scrappy, for one. I felt like I had to fight a little harder to succeed in my career because I am a woman and because I am gay. Likewise, Detroit had been fighting relentlessly to turn itself around since before I arrived, and the populace was fighting right along with it. The grit and determination you'll find here is something that many people remark upon. It inspires me to keep working to improve not only our organization but also the community as a whole. In addition, I am an egalitarian—Detroit has less of an established hierarchy than many other places I've lived. If you appreciate the city and have the requisite respect for its diversity, you can come in and have a voice.

I believed in Detroit and I shared my feelings with anyone who would listen. I think that was the reason Detroiters gravitated toward me and asked me to lead on community boards as soon as I arrived. Over the years, I became involved in the community in a way that was unlike my peers. I was viewed as a leader—not just a health-care leader.

Of course, much of the speaking I did was on behalf of Henry

Ford, in an attempt to change the way the community felt about our industry and its impact on the region. There was a strong belief in Michigan that health care was a liability rather than an asset. We heard the constant refrain: GM spends more on health care than it does on steel; lower health-care costs would have saved the auto industry.

In general, there was considerable criticism and negativity directed at health care. I couldn't understand it and I refused to acquiesce. I knew about communities—like Durham, North Carolina, and Cleveland, Ohio—that viewed health care as a signature industry. They understood its presence to be a true strength because it attracted talent and created access to great health care for individuals and businesses alike. Great health care is an attraction. This became one of my mantras. I would talk about the strength of Henry Ford, but I'd also work to change the perception of health care in general.

Only later, when we went through the 2008–09 bankruptcies of two of our major automotive companies and ultimately the bankruptcy of the city, did it become abundantly clear that health care in Detroit was a major part of the solution for the economic challenges of the city and the state. The jobs would remain as long as health care did. Of course, numerous hospitals fled, but we remained fully committed to Detroit.

At last, we were all on the same page. The reality was that Detroit needed us, just as we needed Detroit in countless ways.

Detroit needed HFHS and other growing businesses in order to start to turn the tide back in the right direction. All told, the number of manufacturing jobs in Detroit proper fell from 296,000 in 1950 to just 27,000 in 2011;[1] and, between 2000 and 2010, the city's population fell by 25 percent, changing its ranking from the nation's tenth-largest city to eighteenth.[2] Following the shift of people and jobs to the suburbs, or to other states or nations, many of the city's neighborhoods became distressed and heavily abandoned. High crime and political corruption were two further weights dragging the city down to the depths.

We couldn't make up that deficit by any means, but we were clearly part of the solution. And as we gained momentum, we were able to help the city more and more. Our employment numbers increased from 12,000 in 1989 to 23,000 in 2015. We began attracting patients to Detroit from all over the world as breakthrough procedures and innovative care made headlines. We became a driver of social and economic revitalization in the region through community partnerships and initiatives, including incentives for Henry Ford employees to live in Midtown Detroit. In other words, we served as a stabilizing factor in the city and a bright light in the region's hope for renewal.

We needed Detroit then and now because we are connected to the city in numerous crucial ways. As a health-care provider we are a community resource for the region we serve. Our greatest limiting factor would be the ongoing decline of the city. Our patients are largely from the region, as is the bulk of our employees. With uncompensated care one of our biggest challenges to profitability, a strong Detroit is essential to our long-term success. As health systems over the years have become more corporatized, many of them have of lost their way in terms of their community focus. That will never be the case with HFHS. We were created by Henry Ford to serve the community, and that emphasis is central to our mission, vision, and values. In fact, today we continue to look for better ways to connect ever more closely with the community. Our role as an employer and an economic force remains central to our strategy, as does our primary vision of transforming lives and communities through health and wellness, one person at a time.

Thinking Differently About Our Role

If the ongoing success of Henry Ford is linked to the stability of Detroit, then leading a coordinated charge to hasten the community's recovery is fully within the scope of our interests. And given our mission and vision around community, the effort is even more appropriate. That said, economic development is not a core competency for most health systems. In fact, it's unconventional for an organization like ours to attempt it in any meaningful way. In order for it to work, we've had to think very differently about our role and about investing in ventures that have nothing to do with health care.

One of the best examples of thinking outside of our usual frame of reference is our partnership with the Detroit Medical Center and Wayne State University to incentivize employees to reside in the city. Launched during the recession, amid automotive industry bankruptcies and massive job loss in Detroit, the program accumulated a pool of $1 million to get started. "Live Midtown" offers cash incentives to employees at any of the three organizations who elect to live in Midtown: it awards $25,000 to those who buy a home, $5,000 to those who renovate a home they already own, $2,000 in year one to those who rent, and $1,000 to those who rent the following year. The first Live Midtown program, launched in January 2011, was instantly successful. It exhausted its funding in seven months and attracted 220 new residents to Midtown Detroit during that time. The program is ongoing, and newer offshoots include incentives to "Live Downtown."

There are a number of other major ways we at HFHS are boosting the local economy and redeveloping Detroit. One is by acquiring property in the neighborhoods around Henry Ford Hospital. As part of that effort, in 2012 we began a $500 million expansion of our Downtown Detroit campus. The vision over the next ten to fifteen years includes expansion of clinical facilities, green space, and commercial, retail, and residential development. As a key part of that effort, we worked with Cardinal Health in 2015 to open a sprawling, state-of-the-art health-care-supply distribution center in the neighborhood. The $30 million Cardinal Health Distribution Center marks a key development in the city's revitalization, bringing 150 jobs to the neighborhood. Part of our contribution was acquiring the eighteen acres of property and performing the planning work, including conducting environmental testing and obtaining proper zoning approvals and development incentives. In order to ensure the success of the venture, we also shifted our entire distribution and warehousing business over to Cardinal Health. The beautiful 275,000-square-foot building transforms an area that, until recently, contained crumbling industrial structures and withering, desolate fields.

We are also part of a consortium that is developing a new light rail system that will run through Detroit, from Downtown to the boulevard where Henry Ford Hospital is located. In this case, we invested $3 million to add a station stop that will serve Henry Ford Hospital and the surrounding neighborhood. This, together with our other economic development efforts, will benefit us as well as the community. But in order to envision that mutual benefit we had to set aside the normal way that we thought about investments to determine what would really connect us to the community.

Beyond pure infrastructure development, we've used innovation and entrepreneurship as a means of fueling growth in Detroit. A community like Detroit, with its considerable grit and determination, is a fertile environment for innovation, and we've witnessed some inspiring successes as new ventures rise up from the ashes of shuttered businesses. In fact, in 1999 we played a leading role in one of the earliest attempts to sponsor start-up ventures in Detroit. In partnership with General Motors and Wayne State University, we incorporated TechTown, an incubator for innovation.

The concept mushroomed rapidly, and, in 2004, a 135,000-square-foot facility was opened in a landmark 1927 Albert Kahn building contributed by General Motors. Today, the building houses TechTown, its incubating enterprises, and other forward-facing Detroit businesses. Our former CFO and current CEO of our health plan, Jim Connelly, has served as treasurer of TechTown since its inception. Its recently renovated first floor is home to thriving business in the retail, wholesale, and technology sectors.[3] TechTown is a dynamic place where talent, technologies, and capital converge. In fact, we put a couple of our major research activities into the building as well, including our genetics work and our drug discovery laboratory. With this move, we're helping to create a space where people can collaborate to drive change. It is something that appeals to young professionals and it has already made a difference in the way Detroit defines itself and in the way it will evolve to succeed in the future.

TechTown is a great beginning, and there is much more to come. In 2014, for instance, I was asked by Detroit mayor Mike Duggan to chair a working group charged with creating an innovation district to accelerate job growth and entrepreneurship in the city. Our seventeen-member advisory committee—in partnership with anchor organizations in Detroit as well as private-sector companies, including those backed by Quicken Loans chairman Dan Gilbert—is examining ways to leverage the assets in Midtown and Downtown in order to tap into the knowledge economy. Our goal is to drive new growth and job creation, and to launch and attract new businesses to vital areas of Detroit. The 4.3-square-mile district under discussion already holds 55 percent of the city's jobs, though it represents only 3.1 percent of its land mass.[4]

This is exciting. And this work lies at the intersection of several areas about which I am enormously passionate—Detroit, innovation, and turnarounds. I am excited to help move this concept forward because I firmly believe that it will support Detroit in evolving and becoming better than ever.

Caring for the Community

If economic development is somewhat new for HFHS, health care is not, and we are preemptive in how we approach serving the community. We need to be extremely disciplined in order to succeed at the job that we were founded to perform. After all, the complex social and economic conditions in Detroit mandate that we operate at peak performance. In addition, federal legislation and insurance reform are pushing health-care delivery organizations away from a fee-for-service model and toward one based on value—higher quality and lower cost. On top of that, altered demographics, from the vast aging population to young millennials with entirely different needs and expectations, put the onus on health systems to be nimble and open to change. Any way that you look at it, this is a perfect storm. And yet, HFHS is on solid ground because we have been paving this path in Detroit for a century. After all, Henry Ford Hospital was founded by a legendary stickler for efficiency—and we have followed his example closely.

We set our community health agenda using a seven-pillar approach to strategy—which in itself is not unusual. Most systems have a stated focus on finance, clinical care, and perhaps even education. But it is unconventional to have a strategic focus on the needs of the community. As part of that focus, our community pillar team analyzes multiple sources of health statistics, demographic data, and socioeconomic information to identify key communities. We use that information to prioritize specific needs and determine the focus of care for underserved and disadvantaged populations.

A specific tool the community pillar team uses to stake out a plan is our Community Health Needs Assessment. We use the triannual federally mandated assessment to help us improve the health of the people we serve through community programs and intervention strategies. The last assessment was completed in 2013, and we have used it to identify programs and services that will have the greatest measurable impact on the people we serve. The 2013 report pointed out areas on which we should focus, including poor access to care/lack of health coverage, obesity, lack of access to healthy food, diabetes, hypertension, and heart disease.

Using the information from the assessment and the anecdotal evidence we collect as a matter of course, we've developed ways to proactively attend to the health of the community and focus on preventive care as well as on reducing readmissions.

Infant Mortality—Creating a Safety Net

In 2007, we began to examine the high rate of infant deaths across the area. Despite the existence of high-quality health systems in metro Detroit, the appalling rates of death among the most vulnerable members of the community—infants—rivaled that of third-world countries. A major driver was the disproportionately high number of deaths among African American infants, who died at a rate that was nearly double the overall rate for the state, according to the Michigan Department of Community Health.[5] The causes included the absence of a coordinated effort to link at-risk women with the necessary medical and social resources. Consequently, the safety net had gaping holes. Because a staggering problem like this requires a concerted effort, we collaborated with competing regional health-care providers to form the Detroit Regional Infant Mortality Reduction Task Force. Our goal was to improve the conditions that lead to infant survival through the first year of life.

The effort partners health systems with community organizations and local health departments to create a comprehensive approach that addresses both clinical and social factors associated with infant mortality. More specifically, the initiative connects at-risk women with "neighborhood navigators" who recruit women in three of the highest-risk neighborhoods in Detroit and connect them to an array of socially and economically appropriate health-care services, local neighborhood resources, and phone- and web-based sources of information to meet their needs. Pregnant women receive intensive intervention, including home visits and mentoring. The program results have reset the bar, and led to zero infant deaths among the enrolled women in at-risk neighborhoods.

The next iteration of this program, which is upcoming, uses the same techniques to connect women and their children with social services and health care, and also creates opportunities for group visits to doctors and counselors, whereby women and their peers join the program together to create a high level of peer support and reinforcement.

Obesity and Malnutrition—Generation with Promise

In 2007, our own Dr. Kimberlydawn Wisdom, the nation's first state-level surgeon general, founded a program called Generation with Promise. Her commitment is to support Michigan's young people, their families, faith-based organizations, and communities through knowledge and skills, to empower them to create communities in which healthy lifestyle choices are the default option. The program aims to help students and their families move more and eat better, changing lives in the process. Drawing on the expertise of registered dietitians, professional chefs, and health educators, local schools and physicians work together to improve healthy behaviors through nutrition education, including cooking demonstrations and food tastings for elementary, middle, and high school students and their families. The interactive approach includes a class on how to feed a family of six a healthy meal on a shoestring budget of $10, after which families receive recipes and $10 food vouchers redeemable at local markets.

Health Screening for Chronic Conditions

The African American Initiative for Male Health Improvement (AIMHI) is a joint effort of the U.S. Office of Minority Health and HFHS—started many years ago to provide screening and education for African American men at high risk for diabetes, hypertension, and other diseases, and to help them access care and improve their overall health. In support of the program, Dr. Wisdom went into the community on the weekends, visiting barbershops, churches, and community centers to enroll people. AIMHI transcends the conventional approach of public health screening programs by moving participants from disease recognition into treatment, and empowers them to manage their chronic conditions. After many years, it has become a signature program that underscores Henry Ford's connection to the African American community of Detroit.

Finding Common Ground

Numerous programs, in addition to those above, are ongoing. From school-based health clinics and the Henry Ford Early College to health-care kiosks in churches and community centers, our community outreach and economic development efforts have partnership as their common denominator. For economic development, we partner with public and private organizations, including our competitors, as well as with entrepreneurs and small businesses. In our community, we partner with health-care and social service organizations and state and federal government, as well as thousands of members of the Detroit community.

I first started partnering with community organizations years ago in Akron when I was creating a program to reach out to the elderly in their homes. In this case, I partnered with a local community group so we didn't have to fund all of the required infrastructure on our own. The group had a call center and other resources that I needed, and we had healthcare resources for seniors in the community.

Both in Akron and in Detroit I found that the key to effective partnering is finding common ground—of which there is plenty. If you find that common ground, you can transcend barriers such as competitive interests. To offer one example: for years I've met regularly with a group of fellow health-care CEOs from across southeast Michigan. We get together every few months to talk about ways to work together. These are our competitors and yet we share ideas and resources because our needs overlap in a multitude of ways. We always find common ground and a reason to collaborate.

It's also important to create a partnership mentality within an organization. You need first to be aligned with your board, of course. Next, your leadership team must be aligned around a common vision regarding community needs. One of the biggest goals we are all aligned around at HFHS is reinvesting in our Detroit hospital and the Detroit community. We all agree that we need to take smart risks to encourage people to come to Detroit for care, and we need to work with other anchor organizations in Detroit to create a path to renewal.

When you're in Detroit, you have to lead with a lot of heart. It is not always an easy place to be, but there is no place I believe could be more rewarding. We have been able to grow despite Detroit's shrinking population, and I credit that to our strong connection to the community. We have been able to innovate and drive social and economic revitalization in the region through community partnerships and initiatives because other people care about the success of Detroit as much as we do. We have been able to attract high-caliber staff and physicians because they share a passion for Detroit and a mission for innovative care. I always tell people: if you're looking for easy, this isn't it. If you're looking to make a difference in the community, to reap incredible rewards, to innovate and continue to grow, and to work with a phenomenal team of people, then this is the place you want to be.

CHAPTER EIGHT

Face the Future

I can't walk away from difficult situations—it's simply not in my nature. Throughout my career, I have always observed trying times through a problem-solving lens and asked: "What's broken and how can I fix it?" That focus on anticipating problems and fixing faults is part of the reason we have been able to sustain our financial performance through thick and thin at Henry Ford. It's the reason we've grown over a thirteen-year period in which Michigan lost a million jobs and Detroit lost population, grappled with a major economic collapse and fiscal bankruptcy.

Despite our success, we've done a lot of very hard things during my tenure. We closed three hospitals and orchestrated a turnaround of the entire system. We cut costs radically and made difficult choices about jobs and programs. We even "lost" most of the health system's short-term cash. I'll never forget the day in September 2008, when our CFO, Jim Connelly, walked into my office with all of the color drained from his face. He said, "Nancy, I think we have a problem." Jim was a guy who never came to me with problems—he always just solved them—so I knew something was very wrong. At the time, nearly all of the health system's short-term cash was held in the AAA-rated Reserve Primary Fund. It was the oldest money market account in the country and was considered to be an extremely safe place to invest working cash. Then the financial world turned on its head. Lehman Brothers collapsed as part of the credit default debacle of 2008. There was a run on the fund, and the bank froze it. We couldn't access the short-term cash we needed to pay employees and vendors. Jim told me this, and the next thing he said was, "But we're working the problem. We're talking with the banks. We're going to figure out some short-term fixes." We got most of our money back eventually, but it took years of legal wrangling and jumping a lot of hurdles.

Nobody likes being confronted with such difficult situations. Yet these are the challenges that keep me coming back: I want to see things through and be part of the solution. So even I was surprised when a critical situation prompted me to realize it was time to retire from the health system. The crisis came during our near-miss merger with Beaumont Health System in 2013. We had completed a tremendous amount of due diligence on the deal and were partway through the integration work. The public announcements had been made, and we were gearing up to see the deal through. And yet, I had come to the conclusion that the merger was a mistake for Henry Ford. Our cultures were too different, and I could see no way that we could merge with Beaumont Health without losing the critical attributes that made us so unique and successful. It also had become personal for me, and the stress was affecting my health. I was willing to step aside promptly, however, if our board believed that the merger was a good strategic move for the organization.

At that point, on a sunny Sunday morning in May 2013, I called Sandy Pierce, chair of the Henry Ford board, and board member Bill Ford, great-grandson of Henry Ford and the executive chairman of Ford Motor Company, and told them that I was ready to retire. These are both people I trust, admire, and with whom I have had an exceptional working relationship. I said to them, "If there needs to be someone else leading this company, someone who can get behind this merger, I'm ready to start the process now. I don't want to be the problem."

This was a turning point in the deal. Sandy and Bill, as well as Chief Operating Officer Bob Riney and a number of others, were similarly convinced that the merger was a cultural misfit that could destroy Henry Ford. That, of course, was the last thing any of us wanted. On that same Sunday, Sandy and Bill called a meeting with me, and others including Bob Riney and board member David Hempstead. They told me they wanted me to be the CEO more than they wanted the merger to be completed. At that time they asked me, "Can you stay with us long enough to put a solid succession in place?" I said, "I will do that. I will not leave Henry Ford in the lurch."

At that point, I started thinking in earnest about how to lead the succession process. It was an important moment in my life as I considered my future and what I was going to do next. That's when it really sunk in for me. It was time to retire from Henry Ford, and I would leave with the company strong rather than in a position where it could possibly backslide financially. In order to do that, I needed to see us through some difficult situations. The first was shutting down HFHS's merger with Beaumont Health System.

The Beaumont Merger

The Henry Ford–Beaumont merger was part of a broader trend of health-care consolidation occurring nationwide. In general, the recent surge in hospital mergers is due to new financial incentives, federal reimbursement cuts, and cost containments that are part of the Affordable Care Act.[1] This means that scale matters more than ever in health care. It's one of the reasons we focused so heavily on growth since I became chief executive and why I am so pleased that we were able to double in size from $2.2 billion to nearly $5 billion in annual revenue. Scale creates cost efficiencies and the ability to achieve better reach. Building a new hospital and acquiring two others, combined with the additional growth in our health system, allowed us to fill our geographic footprint and spread fixed costs across a larger base. Scale is considered an important element of strategy in health care, and if the merger had gone through, the resulting hospital system would have been one of the largest in the Unites States.

Beaumont approached us in the spring of 2012. We received a letter from a third-party financial firm, Kaufman Hall, soliciting our bid to partner with Beaumont and potentially bring it into our system. At that time, Beaumont was about half our size in terms of total revenue and two-thirds our size based on the delivery system. Although we were larger and had a construct that included a six-hundred-thousand-member Health Alliance Plan, Beaumont was the dominant player in the affluent northern suburban markets of Detroit. Both systems were financially sound overall and, despite some facility overlap, were fairly complementary in terms of geographic coverage. The merger would have been one of equals rather than an acquisition of one system by the other. I told Sandy Pierce about the letter at the Baldrige awards ceremony in Washington, DC. While the proposal came as a surprise to her, just as it did to many of us, it was something we decided we had to explore.

We kept the idea under wraps that summer in order to undertake the initial due diligence and start our internal vetting process. The potential merger was a closely held secret, known only to a very small group of senior leaders at Henry Ford and Beaumont. We went on to make a series of presentations to Beaumont's board and were successful in moving through consecutive levels of scrutiny. On October 31, 2012, we announced that we signed a letter of intent with Beaumont to combine our operations into a new $6.4 billion organization. We shared the news with Henry Ford employees and physicians, and then we went public in the media with a joint press conference.

I think most people were excited by the merger prospect. I know that I was—the strategic aspect of the plan was clear and compelling. It would give us incredible strength in every part of the metro Detroit market. But I was nervous, as well, because the cultures of the two organizations were so different. We anticipated potential conflicts, in part because we would have two hospitals within a few miles of each other in the northern Macomb and northern Oakland County areas of Detroit. And, we suspected, there was resistance to our commitment to service in the city of Detroit, as Beaumont was not accustomed to managing the high levels of uncompensated care that come with a large impoverished urban environment. Finally, we had two significantly different physician organizations: Beaumont doctors were in private practice, whereas a large number of our physicians were salaried as part of the Henry Ford Medical Group.

After seven months of planning and exploration, many of the troubling issues that emerged early on became major concerns. The first issue was Beaumont's governance model. The CEO was relatively new and the board chairman worked sixty hours a week, overseeing business operations from an office in the C-suite. That was not a model to which I was accustomed. I had been Henry Ford's CEO for almost ten years by then, and our board had full confidence in me. I managed operations independently and board members oversaw higher-level strategy and policy decisions. When I met Beaumont's board chair I was frank with him, saying that it was not my desire to operate that way, and I think that made him very uncomfortable. Second, it became apparent to us that members of the Beaumont medical staff did not support the merger. They, along with some of Beaumont's senior leadership, seemed to be testing or judging our organization, criticizing our model as well as our mission and values, rather than objectively evaluating us based on the original premise of our plans to merge. They had approached us, after all, so their apparent lack of enthusiasm was troubling. Finally, it became clear, based on some of their frank remarks, that our focus on Detroit, and on diversity in general, was an issue. We were not an organization that would waver in terms of our commitment to the city, and ultimately that was an important imperative they did not share.

Two radically different perspectives emerged for the would-be organization. I think Beaumont realized this around the same time we did. Many of the foundational elements in the letter of intent, including the preservation of two academic medical centers in Detroit and

Royal Oak, were no longer supported by some of Beaumont's leaders. Ultimately, we did not share the same values, vision of where health care was going, or desire to drive change and create new models. A couple of months following that pivotal Sunday meeting, when I had offered to retire, we pulled the plug. We announced that we were walking away from the deal.

Seeing Things Through

Pulling away from the Beaumont merger was a defining moment for us. It was a difficult experience and it took a while for us to recover, yet it was clear that we emerged stronger. We understood our strengths, reaffirmed our values, and recognized that our vision of health care was different from that of other organizations. That different vision is a strength for us, and we value it highly. Interestingly, we heard sighs of relief from many physicians, employees, and even a few patients— people seemed afraid that we would lose what is special about HFHS if the deal went through. Whether that would have occurred is debatable, but we walked away with a certainty about the special aspects of our organization that we are committed to. And the process also helped us gain a better understanding of Beaumont and its competitive strengths. When you get that far inside a competing organization you're afforded a glimpse of the way its leaders think and act, and have an opportunity to learn from their strengths as they learned about us. That's a pretty unique opportunity, and it broadened our scope. We often factor that knowledge into our strategic decisions.

The pre-merger process also showed us how strong we really are. We need to be—not only because of the complexities of our industry, and of Detroit, but also because speed bumps occur with regularity. Not every challenge will be quite like the Beaumont deal, but difficulties will continue to confront us nonetheless. Since the failed merger, we weathered a challenging eighteen months installing an advanced electronic medical record (EMR) and billing system across all of Henry Ford. Nearly twenty-five years ago, Henry Ford was one of the first hospital systems to use electronic patient records in an ambulatory setting to ensure quality and patient safety. The new EMR builds upon that early information system to transform the way we provide care for patients. The initiative required a $350-million financial investment (including between $50 and $75 million dollars a year in additional operating costs) and thousands of IT and training hours, entailing considerable cost cutting and a level of disruption and distraction for physicians and employees that was truly profound. That financial commitment came at a time of reduced patient volume—associated with the lower readmission rate brought about by health-care reform—creating a lot of economic stress on the system.

All of these challenges tested our mettle, but we made it through better than ever. In fact, 2015 is turning out to be the system's best financial year on record. That is gratifying for all of us as Henry Ford Hospital celebrates one hundred years, and as I celebrate my final year as chief executive at Henry Ford Health System. One of the rewards of never walking away from a difficult situation is being able to retire when the health system is at the top of its game and the best it has ever been.

Naming a Successor

I was forty-eight when I was appointed chief executive at Henry Ford. Fourteen years later, I am retiring at age sixty-two. Personally, I think a forty-eight-year-old CEO who retires at sixty-two represents a fairly youthful paradigm. And I believe that's the way it should be.

Being a CEO requires an intense focus on strategic thinking and operational performance. Although I remain as committed as ever to our vision, I know that I have a little less wherewithal than I did five years ago. It's not about losing your way—you simply lose some of your steam because it's hard to sustain focus for a prolonged period of time. In my career, I've always felt that eight to ten years was the right span of time to remain in a position. At Henry Ford, I had a chance to do multiple jobs, and I believe that allowed me to remain longer. The challenges, as well, have been motivating and constant.

Clearly, any CEO searching for a successor hopes to find someone who can continue what she started and take the organization to the next level. Yet, succession is hard to get right, and even the best-laid plans can go awry. I'm living proof of that. Before coming to HFHS, I returned to Akron, Ohio, to succeed my old boss and mentor, Al Gilbert, and run a health system I knew very well. It was a tremendous opportunity. Then I received the call from Gail Warden, and very quickly, with Al's encouragement, I was relocating to Detroit instead of staying in Akron. Al, unfortunately, was left to rethink his succession plan. This happens frequently: candidates get other opportunities; the pool of individuals qualified to lead large, complex organizations is extremely small; and companies often have multiple internal candidates vying for the top slot, which can be immensely disruptive.

When Kathy Oswald joined the organization as chief human resource officer, in 2007, she brought a skill set around succession planning and leadership development that we had previously not had. Internally, she put systems into place that allowed us to identify high-potential individuals interested in leadership who were ready, following developmental opportunities, for more senior roles. She also created an advanced leadership academy to offer senior leaders a broader view of the industry, including the financing and delivery aspects of health systems and the realities of running a big system. While I am a huge proponent of internal promotion, I was relatively certain that an external candidate was needed at HFHS when I retired.

After I spoke to the board about staying on for a few years, they asked me to identify external candidates. I asked for Kathy's help and we began looking around the country. She had built a solid executive search capability within her division, and understood that certain qualities were essential for the next CEO of Henry Ford. I've been around this field long enough to know most of the top leaders in health care. I also recognize, as well as anyone, the unique challenges of leading an organization like ours. We weren't looking for someone who was accustomed to a suburban organization in a growing market with three hundred days of cash on hand. It is a much greater challenge to grow in a market that is flat or in decline. Added to that is the fact that few organizations in the country have a very large group practice, a health plan, an academic medical center, a safety net responsibility to the population, and an anchor position in a vulnerable community. I wanted someone who had a track record of success. I also wanted someone who was committed to an urban, diverse patient population, and who was dedicated to taking our quality journey with Baldrige to the next level.

After a few misses, I found that person through happenstance and good fortune. Wright Lassiter III was CEO of Alameda Health System in Oakland, California. We met briefly in Washington, DC, when we were both on a panel of four individuals at the inaugural "U.S. News Hospital of Tomorrow" leadership forum in October of 2013. We were talking about creativity and innovation in the urban environment and the impact of the Medicaid expansion and the Affordable Care Act. He got up to talk, and I was blown away. I have heard a lot of people in health care speak, but I have not heard many people speak with as much passion and creativity around these issues.

I went back to my hotel room after the talk and did a search to find out more about him. What I found supported my hunch. He had taken a troubled organization and turned it around, essentially rebuilding a hospital through acquisitions and improvements, and remade it into Alameda Health System. Wright had distinctive ideas that were deeply insightful, and he was recognized around the country as a talented leader, having been named one of the "Top 25 Minority Executives in Healthcare" by *Modern Healthcare*. He also understood complexity and was committed to providing top-notch health care for people in a vulnerable community. Essentially, he took on a very tough assignment in Oakland, when he could've gone a different way, and he made it work.

I was struck by my early impression of Wright's leadership capabilities and his accomplishments. Even though Wright would not necessarily have been on our radar, because he ran a smaller organization, I thought, "Wow, this is a person who could really do the job."

I told Kathy about Wright, and she began the due diligence process. After she came back with a very positive response, I spent time talking with him and subsequently went out to visit him in Oakland. We had an excellent dinner and I spent the better part of the following day meeting with Wright and his senior team to learn about what he's done and the important issues he faced. With a public hospital board and a very challenging set of business circumstances, he didn't have an easy job. Despite the fact that the Alameda Health System was much smaller than HFHS, Wright was dealing with significant complexity. We began what turned out to be nearly a year of discussions. Sandy Pierce, chair of the board, went out to meet with him after I did, and she agreed that he seemed like a talented leader who was ready for this type of opportunity.

The courtship process is always interesting and delicate. Although Wright and his wife, Cathy were not sure they did not want to move to Detroit and brave the brutal winters, we continued to encourage them to visit. If my experience at Henry Ford taught me anything about attracting leaders, it is this: the key to increasing interest is getting individuals to visit. The people and the culture here are extremely special, and if the fit is right, a visit generally seals the deal.

In September 2014, Wright and Cathy came out and spent three days with us. We had the best weather in months that week, despite a horrible winter and a rainy summer. They had dinner one night with Sandy and her husband and Pam and me, and over the next two days Wright met key board members and some of the executive team. As we hoped, Wright became enamored with the organization and the opportunity to lead it. Most importantly, Cathy became comfortable enough with the community that she said to Wright, "This is what you're supposed to do next. I can see it. I can see it in your eyes, I can see it with how you're interacting with the folks here. I'm not sure I'm going to love Michigan, but this is where you're supposed to be and I'll support you."

According to Wright, there were three things that made Henry Ford a place he wanted to be. First, there was our vision of an organization that would operate at the top of the game in health care but still maintain humble roots in the community it serves. That was a very big part of the equation for him. Next, he found the plethora of strategic conundrums facing Henry Ford, as well as the numerous opportunities, to be intellectually appealing. The last thing he found appealing, he said, was the opportunity to help lead a major economic force in a community that was experiencing a renaissance. The chance to participate in restoring Detroit was a significant attraction for him. In short, Wright said that it was "wildly appealing to be able to lead an organization that would play a significant role in reestablishing one of America's greatest cities to the successful point."

I think that says it all.

An Unconventional Succession

Succession is a process like any other, and people need to proceed through the stages of change in order to reach acceptance. Bringing Wright on board in the way we did—going outside the usual search process and building in a two-year overlap for Wright and myself—was designed to ease the transition for the organization and for Wright. Did it work that way? I think it did, but let me explain the rationale.

By circumventing the traditional executive search process, we believed we could find the right candidate faster and create a clear pathway for him. Sometimes an organization needs a turnaround effort to get things back on track. That entails a departure from the type of leadership the organization had previously been accustomed to. Yet at other times, a radical shift is not what's needed. At Henry Ford, I got the clear sense from our board and our leadership that we needed to sustain the progress we had made and continue to grow. Given that mandate, I was concerned—and I think our board shared my concern—that the traditional search process would be risky. When you are going out and simply casting the net, the odds of finding the right fish are not great.

Because the stakes were so high, we opted to trust our instincts and maintain a greater degree of control. After all, a large part of success in leadership transitions is achieving the right fit culturally. You can have the smartest leader in the world, but if he is not a good match for the organization, he may fail and the organization may falter. My deep understanding of our culture and the specifics of our environment enabled me to identify Wright as a prime candidate within an hour of hearing him speak. He was running a much smaller organization at the time, so chances are good that he would have slipped through a search firm's net. Yet, after thirteen years of running HFHS, I have a clear sense of the type of person who will thrive here. By bringing on Wright, I could vouch for him, in a sense, and be the one to introduce him and enter his phenomenal past performance into the record. In addition, identifying Wright while I was still part of the organization made people more comfortable with the change because we were able to maintain some sense of familiarity.

We hired Wright as president of the system in December 2014, two years prior to my departure, as a way to buy us time. Extending the transition allowed the board and the rest of the leadership team to learn to work effectively with Wright while I was still on hand to support him. To borrow a metaphor from Dr. Kimberlydawn Wisdom, transitioning from me to Wright is like passing the baton during a footrace. In order to avoid dropping the baton, you run alongside the next runner for many yards before he actually grabs the baton and takes off with it. You don't just throw it to your teammate and expect him to catch it on the fly. In this case, the extended transition created a smoother handoff.

So far, the handoff is smooth indeed, and if our strong performance is any indication, it will almost certainly continue. As I look toward my retirement in December 2016, the sting of stepping away is greatly lessened because I know that I am leaving the organization in such capable hands.

My Hopes for the Future

As I look toward the next chapter of my life, I feel like I'm leaving Henry Ford at the right time—the organization has strong momentum and a special leader will be in place as chief executive. We've become a $5 billion organization with 23,000 employees and more than 89,000 patients admitted to HFHS hospitals annually. We are the fifth-largest employer in metro Detroit and the sixth-largest health system in Michigan. I hope that our considerable success is ongoing—and I believe that it will be, in large part because of the excellent people we have in place and their commitment to HFHS's mission, vision, and values.

My hope for Detroit is that it continues along its path to renewal and that the health-care sector, and Henry Ford in particular, continues to play a role in restoring the city to greatness. Judging by the number of new tech companies, investments in the arts and sports, the significant increases in venture capital and federal research grants, and the soaring pride of longtime residents of Midtown and Downtown Detroit, the city is, once again, full of possibility and poised for future growth and momentum.

In health care, I hope that we can understand our patients better and engage them at a much deeper level. The cultural complexity of our world means that everyone's needs are different, and I hope that we can create a customized approach to health care that takes diversity into account. There's also significant work ahead to determine how to pay for high-quality, reliable care in this country. I hope that we can continue to innovate and devise new and better models for delivery and financing.

I also hope that women and minorities fill more top positions in health systems and large organizations in every sector. I have no doubt that business will become a better place with greater diversity in leadership that fully reflects the global world we live and work in. This will require systemic changes, as well as a personal commitment from individual leaders to focus intentionally on equity and diversity.

Turning to my future, I also have a number of hopes for myself. One, which is very personal, is to take better care of myself: to exercise, have fun, and build into my life the hobbies I enjoy. I think that will help me stay in better shape and hopefully live a little bit longer.

The second thing I hope is that I can remain intellectually engaged through board service, teaching, community service, and other special projects. I want to serve on a number of different types of boards, for instance, and move beyond health care. As a lifelong learner, I have enjoyed getting to know organizations such as Walgreens and the Kresge Foundation as I've served on their boards. The next part of intellectual engagement, for me, is through teaching. I hope to continue to teach—probably at the University of Michigan and Cornell—on at least a part-time basis. Finally, I hope and expect to be involved in helping children within the community of Detroit and elsewhere.

My hope for Michigan is that it becomes more hospitable for its LGBT citizens. Pam and I hope to stay in Michigan for both personal and professional reasons, yet we need to live in a place where we feel comfortable. We are, frankly, disappointed in Michigan's current lack of support for the LGBT community. There are too many examples of the state making poor decisions, in my view, including our governor's recent signing of a law that essentially allows discrimination against LGBT people. It's a disappointing development, but I realize we can either stay and try to make a difference or retreat. We'd like to stay. We have a wonderful circle of friends and family here, including both our dads. In addition, we've felt tremendously supported at Henry Ford and elsewhere—there are a lot of enlightened people in Michigan, and certainly in Detroit.

Finally, I also hope to contribute in a public service capacity. In the spring of 2015, I received a call from Sloan Gibson, the deputy secretary of Veterans Affairs, to say that President Obama was interested in appointing me to the Commission on Care, established by Congress to examine ways to best deliver health care to military veterans. He asked me questions about my background, and I said that what I really like to do is make organizations better. I was a chief operating officer for twenty years, and I'm very operationally focused. I think he liked what he heard, because he called back in a week or so and asked if I would be willing to chair the commission. It's not an honor I expected, but the timing is ideal, with Wright on board, and the opportunity dovetails perfectly with my interests. I also believe it reflects well on HFHS to have me serve in this capacity.

I am proud of what I have accomplished in my career, although I believe that health-care leaders have to put a foot on the gas pedal and be willing to be unconventional if health care is to improve. I got into health-care to make it better—it's always been a labor of love for me. And if I hadn't gotten into health care, I always thought I'd be an orchestra conductor. As a young violinist, I loved watching conductors. I found it amazing that they always knew what everybody was doing. They managed every part of the orchestra—every musician and every instrument that needed to chime in to create beautiful music. I've talked about this for years, and people look at me and say, "Nancy, you *are* leading the orchestra!"

It has been a different sort of orchestra, but one that nonetheless brought together many different sights and sounds. When I think of the people I have met over the years in leadership and the situations we've weathered together, I see how the arc of my career comes together in a sort of musical score, and I hope that I have been the sort of conductor who helped people perform at their best.

NOTES

Introduction

1. This quote always makes me think about Maya Angelou. It is frequently attributed to her in books and other publications. For example, *USA Today* listed the source as an "interview for *Beautifully Said Magazine* (2012)" here: http://www.usatoday.com/story/news/nation-now/2014/05/28/maya-angelou-quotes/9663257/. However, the original source, if it exists, is unknown to me.
2. Sara Ellison and Wallace P. Mullin, "Diversity, Social Goods Provision, and Performance in the Firm," *Journal of Economics and Management Strategy* 23, no. 2 (Summer 2014): 465–481; and "Connecting Corporate Performance, and Gender Diversity," Catalyst, 2004, accessed August, 3, 2015, http://www.catalyst.org/system/files/The_Bottom_Line_Connecting_Corporate_Performance_and_Gender_Diversity.pdf.

Chapter 1

1. "Women CEOs of the S&P 500," Catalyst, April 3, 2015, accessed August 3, 2015, http://www.catalyst.org/knowledge/women-ceos-sp-500.

Chapter 2

1. In 2013, we fell slightly short of profitability due to the installation of a new $350-million electronic medical record system.

Chapter 3

1. Ralph Waldo Trine and Henry Ford, *The Power That Wins: Henry Ford and Ralph Waldo Trine in an Intimate Talk on Life—the Inner Thing—the Things of the Mind and Spirit—and the Inner Powers and Forces That Make for Achievement* (Indianapolis, IN: Bobbs-Merrill Company, 1929), 147.

2. Jeffrey L. Rodengen, *Henry Ford Health System: A 100 Year Legacy*, (Ft. Lauderdale, FL, 2014), 223.

3. Rodengen, *Henry Ford Health System,* 224–225.

4. Rodengen, *Henry Ford Health System,* 220.

5. Henry Ford and Samule Crowther, *My Life and Work* (Garden City, New York: Garden City Publishing Company, Inc., 1922), 83.

6. "Depression Care Program Eliminates Suicide," Henry Ford Health System, accessed August 3, 2015, http://www.henryford.com/body.cfm?id=46335&action=detail&ref=1104.

7. Sabrina Rodak, "6 Steps to Encourage Patient Safety Innovation at Hospitals," Becker's Hospital Review, October 1, 2012, accessed August 3, 2015, http://www.beckershospitalreview.com/hospital-physician-relationships/6-steps-to-encourage-patient-safety-innovation-at-hospitals.html.

8. This is something that William Conway, Henry Ford Medical Group CEO and Chief Quality Officer HFHS, has talked about quite a bit.

9. Tara Parker-Pope, "Making Hospitals Pay for Their Mistakes," *New York Times*, December 19, 2007, accessed August 3, 2015, http://well.blogs.nytimes.com/2007/12/19/making-hospitals-pay-for-their-mistakes/?_r=1.

Chapter 4

1. Henry Ford, *The Great To-Day and Greater Future* (New York: Cosimo, 2006), 66.

2. Henry Ford, *The Great To-Day and Greater Future*, 66.

3. Bill Taylor, "One Hospital's Radical Prescription for Change," *Harvard Business Review*, June 2, 2010, accessed August 3, 2015, https://hbr.org/2010/06/going-radical-one-hospitals-p/.

4. The 3-D printing efforts in cardiology are led by William O'Neill, MD, and the Structural Heart Team at HFHS.

5. StatChat was created by two HFHS doctors: Dr. Ogochukwu Azuh and Dr. Peter Adams.

Chapter 5

1. Ford published an anti-smoking book in 1914: *The Case Against the Little White Slaver* (Detroit: Henry Ford, 1914, revised 1916).

Chapter 6

1. The latest breakdown by ethnicity and nationality dates back to the 2010 census: http://quickfacts.census.gov/qfd/states/26/2622000.html.

2. Christopher P. Scheitle and Roger Finke, *Places of Faith: A Road Trip Across America's Religious Landscape* (New York: Oxford University Press, 2012), 174.

Chapter 7

1. Jeff Green and Mark Clothier, "U.S. Automakers Thrive as Detroit Goes Bankrupt," *Bloomberg News*, July 19, 2013, http://www.bloomberg.com/news/articles/2013-07-19/u-s-automakers-thrive-as-detroit-goes-bankrupt, accessed August 3, 2015.
2. John Wisely and Todd Spangler, "Motor City Population Declines 25%," *USA Today*, March 24, 2011, accessed August 3, 2015, http://usatoday30.usatoday.com/news/nation/census/2011-03-22-michigan-census_N.htm.
3. "TechTown of Detroit, History," accessed August 3, 2015, http://techtowndetroit.org/about-us/history/.
4. Natalie Broda, "Detroit Launches Innovation District to Spur Job Growth," *Detroit News*, June 12, 2014, accessed August 3, 2015, http://www.crainsdetroit.com/article/20140612/NEWS/140619939/detroit-launches-innovation-district-to-spur-job-growth.
5. Steven Ross Johnson, "Mothers' Helpers: Providers, Insurers Use Home Visits to Reduce Infant Mortality," *Modern Healthcare*, March 14, 2015, http://www.modernhealthcare.com/article/20150314/MAGAZINE/303149941.

Chapter 8

1. Moses Harris, "Henry Ford-Beaumont Merger May Have Been Doomed by Good Financial Health," *Detroit Free Press*, May 27, 2013, accessed August 3, 2015, http://www.freep.com/article/20130527/BUSINESS06/305280010/Henry-Ford-Beaumont-failed-hospital-merger.

INDEX

ACKNOWLEDGMENTS

Writing a book was my mother Elizabeth's dream, something I never thought I would do. When she made me write book reports for her during my summer vacation in elementary school, I thought it was pretty cruel. However, although she has been gone for twenty years now, I have heard her voice of encouragement throughout the process of creating this book. My father, John, has always been my staunchest cheerleader, especially when the chips were down. Nothing pleases me more than still having him in my life as my book is completed.

There are countless people who have been central to my leadership journey and who have allowed my unconventional leadership style to flourish, but my inspiration has always come from the employees and physicians I have had the privilege of working with over my career. Their belief in me drove me to take risks, overcome obstacles, and always make decisions with them in mind.

You can never survive as an unconventional leader, however, without supportive mentors, bosses, and colleagues. I have been truly blessed to have exceptional role models and mentors, leadership colleagues, and community partners, especially during my years in Detroit. Gail Warden, Al Gilbert, Allan Gilmour, Gary Valade, Sandy Pierce, and the Ford Family (especially Martha Ford, Bill Ford, and Lynn Ford Alandt) have encouraged me to lead with boldness, but have always had my back during the tough times. Bob Riney, Jim Connelly, Bill Conway, Kathy Oswald, Rose Glenn, Edie Eisenmann, John Popovich, Joe Schmitt, Bill Schramm, Mark Kelley, and the late

Tom Groth were faithfully at my side during many difficult days as we turned around, moved forward, thought differently, and stepped over landmines to achieve greatness at Henry Ford. These colleagues have provided extraordinary leadership, new ideas, and passion and have been a constant source of strength for me.

I have also had the pleasure of working with many innovators, in addition to those already mentioned. These are people who really put themselves "out there," and made me feel confident that we could take risks and make big bets that would pay off—and they always did pay off! Mani Menon, Scott Dulchavsky, Kimberlydawn Wisdom, Dick Zarbo, Bill O'Neill, Mark Coticchia, and Gerard Van Grinsven have made me look really good due to their brilliance and vision.

My "inner circle" for the book has been incredibly important, and has made the process really enjoyable. Rose Glenn has been so helpful in every way, providing her literary expertise, her enthusiasm, and her support for all aspects of the project. She initiated the contact with Carolyn Monaco, who introduced us to Jacque Murphy, and the journey began. Carolyn has been a wonderful advisor and champion of my book, and Jacque has been the best writing partner and friend possible. To fit book writing into my already busy schedule was only accomplished because of the amazing support of my executive assistants, Kim Raniszeski and Yvonne Moyer, who not only made it happen, but also transitioned their jobs during this period, and provided daily encouragement that I should really do this! I have also been so fortunate to work with an innovative and talented publishing company, Bibliomotion, Inc. Erika Heilman, cofounder and publisher, and Alicia Simons, senior director of marketing, have been incredible to work with, and have taught me how to be an effective author.

The most important inspiration for this book has been my partner, Pam. Pam wrote her own book, *Peace at Work*, a couple of years ago, and has been a great supporter of the time and effort I have put into this process. She has also provided vital insights and objectivity during the editing of the manuscript, and she makes my life wonderful every day.